The Lost Civilization of Petra

For Orna

Udi Levy

The Lost Civilization of Petra

Floris Books

Translated by Christian von Arnim

First published in 1996 under the title *Die Nabatäer.*
Versunkene Kultur am Rande des Heiligen Landes
by Verlag Urachhaus, Stuttgart
First published in English in 1999 by Floris Books

British Library CIP Data available

ISBN 0-86315-298-8

Printed in Great Britain
by Bath Press Colourbooks, Glasgow

Contents

CONTENTS

Foreword

Archeological excavations in the whole of the Negev have brought to light the remains of the hitherto forgotten civilization of the Nabateans. The discoveries in Elusa, Mampsis and Avdat opened a fascinating archeological chapter, but although there were many finds, only a few threw any light on the obscurity of Nabatean history. The observation of individual phenomena as practised by archeology, history, and theology has not so far been able to transmit a picture which would accord with the reality of the former life of this people. In order to achieve this, it will be necessary to move away from isolated areas of knowledge and seek a higher standpoint from which all these details meld into a comprehensive picture.

The Nabateans were the descendants of a tribe which migrated from southern Arabia to the deserts by the Mediterranean coast in the sixth century BC. They developed from a typical nomadic tribe into an advanced multi-ethnic civilization. The role of the civilizations or peoples of antiquity is mostly measured by their ability to influence other cultures. The 'classical' examples are the Greek and Roman civilizations.

The unique phenomenon represented by Nabatean culture was not only the existence of a civilization in the desert for more than a millennium; it was a civilization which was able — without giving up its own identity — to integrate influences from other cultures into its own.

The striking feature about this civilization is its masterly handling of such scarce life-supporting resources as exist in the desert. Their management of water and natural growth was unique — as was their development of the trade routes traversing the desert and the avoidance of trade by sea. Military conflict was avoided as much as possible.

Although the Nabateans had an army, it was almost never used for expansionist purposes.

Nabatean culture developed from a nomadic religion which carried its gods with it into a settled Christian civilization in which ethnic and racial origins no longer played any role. Familiar with the concept of resurrection since the second millennium BC, this religion found its conclusion in Christianity via the resurrection cults of the Petran holy sites.

A tribal society managed the transition to a largely democratic monarchy, and from a monarchy to the voluntary relinquishment of political sovereignty, leading to the unique prosperity of an agricultural desert civilization.

The climax of Nabatean artistic creation is represented without doubt by the monumental Petran architecture. Yet the multiplicity of artistic expression of Nabatean civilization is just as amazing as other aspects of this people: a completely new style was created by the assimilation of various influences from neighbouring civilizations.

The proximity to Judea revealed a polar relationship in almost all respects. The absolute ethnocentric attitude of the Judeans was totally absent among the Nabateans, the constant Judean need to defend oneself in the mountains, was superfluous in the desert. The need to preserve religious traditions manifested itself among the Nabateans in an extraordinary capacity of religious metamorphosis.

The present study is an attempt to depict the essence of one of the most mysterious civilizations of the classical world by drawing on the results of all relevant scientific disciplines. The objective of coming to a comprehensive view based firmly on existing research findings requires a constant balancing act between 'how it really was' and 'how it might have been.' It is an approach modelled on the method used by Rudolf Steiner in his historical studies. In doing so, some of the elements which contribute to this outline of the essence of Nabatean civilization should be understood as consciously posed hypotheses and questions.

The temptation to indulge in a detailed description which includes as many particulars as possible, is as great as the challenge to create a comprehensive portrayal of Nabatean civilization. The phenomena to be included therefore had to be strictly selected. The study refrains from a detailed description of all accessible Nabatean sites, with the exception of Petra and Shivta. Instead, aspects are consciously focused on which have receive little or no attention in the other literature. But there are limits to a portrayal such as this one in other respects as well. No description can convey the impression of a summer sunset above the ruins of Shivta, the absolute silence and absence of people, the idea that thousands of people lived here, or the majesty of the Petran monuments.

I would like to express my heartfelt thanks to my wife Orna and our children Juwal, Elijah, Dania and Noam for their patience and support during the writing of this book. Thanks are due also to Winfried Altmann, without whom it would not have been written, my colleague Christine Talker-Jordanis for her illustrations, and Manfred Christ for revision of the manuscript. I wish to express my very special gratitude to Professor Avraham Negev who at all times was prepared to answer my questions.

In conclusion, allow me to add a personal remark. When I started writing this book, it was still inconceivable that it would ever be possible for an Israeli citizen to visit Petra. In the autumn of 1994 I was finally able to fulfil my dream after peace had been concluded between Jordan and Israel. Perhaps I was in a similar situation to the inhabitants of East Berlin who were able to see the Brandenburg Gate from the West for the first time after the collapse of the Wall. For the first time since the seventh century, when the Islamic invasion took place, most of the territory of the former Nabatean kingdom is now accessible to everyone without danger or hindrance.

CHAPTER ONE

Approach to a Forgotten Civilization

The Holy Land stretches from the source of the Jordan to the Red Sea, from the Mediterranean coast to the Dead Sea. Numerous silent ruins, scattered over the whole of the Holy Land, bear witness to the extremely turbulent events which on no few occasions played a key role in determining the course of human history.

Galilee, the northern part of Israel, consists of fertile and gentle hill country, but the landscape becomes harsher and severer in its impact the further south we go in the direction of Jerusalem. This city lies on a rise of the hill country of Judea exactly on the line formed by a watershed. The western slopes are covered by coniferous forests, the eastern ones are bare and stony with little rainfall. They drop in stages to the Dead Sea which lies completely enclosed in a desert landscape. Jerusalem was destroyed nineteen times, and equally often rebuilt. This city, like no other, was the scene of key events and the consequences of some of these affect us to this day.

If we take ourselves back to Biblical times, we encounter Melchizedek, the first priest-king mentioned in the Bible, offering bread and wine to Abraham, founding father of the Jewish people, and giving him his blessing (Gen.14:18). Centuries later, it was again bread and wine which at the same place were to be given ritual and

Figure 1 (overleaf). Wadi Araba, the Edom mountains in the background. The incense road passed by the 'Scorpion Ascent' here in classical times.

sacramental significance for the whole of Christianity. Jerusalem — the place where, in the words of the resident English poet Denis Silk, 'too much time is decanted over too little space.'

Continuing our path southwards, we soon leave the hill country of Judea and cross the magnificent desert landscape of the Negev, stretching to the Gulf of Aqaba. It starts approximately on the level of the East-West line which touches the southern end of the Dead Sea and extends across the widest part of the country. Rarely do people who travel in the Negev to admire the variety of its landscape and natural phenomena know that settlement of the area did not just begin in recent history. Here, too, traces of human activity point to extremely ancient times. But while the history of the northern provinces, and that of Jerusalem in particular, took a changeable and often dramatic course, the chain of historical events in the area south of the Holy Land was much less closely intertwined. The sites where ruins are to be found occur much less frequently in this area than in the north, but their secrets are all the deeper for that.

The following reflections deal with the Negev and its inhabitants, the Nabateans, in the centuries before and after the birth of Christ. The oldest references to the Nabateans come from about the sixth century BC. About a thousand years later, they disappear again from the stage of world history as mysteriously as they arrived. They left little evidence of their mysterious civilization for posterity, and such records as exist pose more riddles today than they give answers.

The Negev desert

The Negev desert bridges the two continents of Africa and Asia. A glance at the map shows an elongated triangle between latitude 20 and 30 N. Each corner touches a different sea. Winter nights are often below freezing, while summer days are over 40 C in the shade.

The northern border forms an imaginary line from the Mediterranean in the west through Beersheba to the southern tip of the Dead Sea. The eastern border is formed by that unique geological formation, the Great Rift Valley, which cuts through the whole eastern part of the Holy Land. The river Jordan follows the northern part running into the Dead Sea at 400 metres below sea level, the lowest point on the surface of the earth. The southern continuation of the rift contains Wadi Araba and the Gulf of Aqaba. The distance from Beersheba to the Red Sea is only 220 km. The western border is less clearly defined merging into the Sinai desert, roughly along the Israel-Egypt border.

The name *Negev* has biblical origins. It refers to the undefined desert area south of the cultivated land. In Hebrew *Negev* means 'towards the south.' It is interesting to note its frequent association with Yemen, the Saba of old. In the original directions for building the tabernacle it reads literally: 'And you shall make upright frames for the tabernacle of acacia wood ... twenty frames for the Negev-Yemen side' (Exod.26:16–18).

Following the course of the Jordan river from Mount Hermon to the Dead Sea, the decrease in vegetation is a clear reflection of the rainfall pattern. With an annual rainfall of 1200 mm Galilee has enough to be clad in a profusion of lush green. Latitude 31 , just south of Beersheba forms the southernmost border of arable land. Usually the desert begins where the rainfall is below 300 mm. Before running its course, the River Jordan reaches desert landscapes, and dies into the Dead Sea where the annual rainfall is under 100 mm (see Map 3).

The northern border of the Negev runs through Beersheba which lies on a wadi carrying the floodwater off the hills of Hebron, the southernmost part of Judea. In antiquity this wadi formed the border between Judea and Nabatea; here were the Roman fortresses which secured the south-eastern border of the empire. Later, when the Nabatean kingdom was under Roman sovereignty it was the border between the provinces of *Palaestina Secunda* (Judea) and *Palaestina Salutaris* (Nabatea).

Already in the fourth millennium BC, long before the Judeans or Nabateans came here, there were people living in the area. The fact that there was human settlement in this area at such an early time, raises the question whether there were climatic changes which subsequently allowed the desert to creep northwards. There is some evidence that there may have been such a climatic shift in the fourth millennium BC. This would have had far-reaching effects, allowing agriculture without artificial irrigation; a technique not developed at that time. This is possibly also a reason why there was no settlement in the Negev in the following two thousand years. Only from about 1200 BC (the time the children of Israel left Egypt) do we find evidence of some settlement, in the form of forts between Beersheba and the Gulf of Aqaba. After the sixth century BC, the region was again uninhabited.

South of the plain of Beersheba there is a region of hills which was the geographic centre of Nabatean civilization. It is a region of strange geological formations giving a glimpse into the formation of the earth. There are three large craters surrounded by high cliffs which appeared at the same time as the upheavals which formed the Great Rift Valley. The cliff faces give a clear impression of the various geological layers.

In the west there are extensive dunes formed over thousands of years by the prevailing west wind blowing fine particles of sand from the Sahara desert to the Negev hills. The dunes thus consist of exceptionally fine sand, and have unique flora and fauna.

The further south one goes the drier and rockier the landscape becomes. South of the Ramon crater there is a region which was never settled for any length of time. It is through this region that the old trade routes of the Nabateans run (see Map 5).

In our time, we travel through the Holy Land on an extensive network of roads, we visit its historical sites and linger in the places which are sacred to Jews, Christians and Muslims. All of them are in the northern part of the country. The road between Beersheba in the north and the Red Sea is usually travelled without a stop. Only a few notice the attraction of this landscape which gives such a barren and hostile impression to the passing glance, or the wealth of its natural phenomena which we encounter at every step. Yet anyone who wants to discover the secrets of the desert must be prepared for a *change of attitude*. The rhythm of life here does not accord with the tempo of mass tourism today. Only those who are prepared to acquaint themselves with the region over a longer period of time will become familiar with it, will learn to know its various facets, its innumerable, constantly changing colours, depending on the time of day and the changing light. The blinding sun during the long summer, the short shadows, the preponderance of light earthy colours: all of these things produce a feeling of monotony in many visitors and make it more difficult for the unpractised eye to pick out the details of the landscape. This means that traces of the civilization which once existed in the desert are also often overlooked.

The first Nabatean tribes probably moved into this area, the Negev, in the sixth and fifth centuries BC. They were nomads whose exact geographical origin has still not been determined with any certainty. This marked the beginning of the history of a people and civilization which occupied a special place in classical antiquity. The Nabateans lived in the Negev for over a millennium into the seventh and eight centuries AD. That alone shows the outstanding importance of this civilization: it is a unique example of the cultivation of the desert over an extended period. There were, of course, civilizations in other arid areas in the East which lived in the desert, but such settlements were abandoned after a brief period if there was no agricultural land available, and their cultures never flowered to the extent that the civilization of the Nabateans did. No other people managed to use the few life-supporting resources which the desert reluctantly releases as effectively as the Nabateans did.

In the past, the desert mostly served as a place of refuge during times of persecution, or a place where people went to commune with themselves and for religious contemplation. The solitude of the desert was a source of revelation to many of the great saints and prophets from all religions. People have to rely on their own resources in such an environment. They are no longer cushioned nor do they have all their needs met by nature, but they do have a more intense experience of their own human essence which enables them to rise above nature. It appears that the Nabateans were motivated by both these aspects, but there were certainly other factors involved as well which caused them to settle in the desert.

The ancestors of the Nabateans were nomadic shepherds. They knew the places in the desert where there was sufficient water to enable man and beast to survive even the dry and hot summer months. Reports by Greek historians show that the Nabateans were masters of cistern construction and water catchment. They built subterranean basins to store a part of the heavy rainfall which came down in winter each year. However, such water reservoirs were not just intended to meet daily requirements in times of peace. When danger threatened, they withdrew into the desert while their enemies soon ran out of the water they needed to carry on the pursuit. Accounts also say that the Nabateans did not build houses, drank no wine and did not plant trees. All these activities are incompatible with a nomadic lifestyle and require the return to a specific *place* to cultivate the fields and reap the harvest. Nomads never form a connection with a place, only with the *road*.

The riddle of Nabatean civilization

Sun and water formed the core of the Nabateans' belief. Many characteristics of their religion can be traced back to Persian influences, although it was, in contrast, largely non-figurative. Indeed, in the early stages of development of Nabatean civilization — as they settled in the desert — there was the complete absence of figurative depiction. No images of any kind were created of the deity. In this respect there was a link to the Yahweh cult in Judea. The Nabateans did not develop their own architectural style until the middle of the second century BC. When nomads make the transition to a settled way of life, this is usually accompanied by the construction of permanent housing which copies local building habits. This did not, however, occur with the Nabateans: they began with religious buildings. These buildings, like the later secular ones for habitation, were characterized by a highly developed style.

With time, the former shepherds turned into merchants trading with camel caravans. The demand for incense and myrrh, both for religious and cosmetic purposes, boomed in the Roman Empire. This created an active trade in which these valuable and desirable goods were transported from southern Arabia to the Mediterranean coast on the backs of camels. The majority of Nabatean cities were established along these trade routes. Here they developed a skilled mastery of pottery production, the quality of which far exceeded the goods of neighbouring cultures. This pottery, too, was clearly the product of religious requirement. It was only later that objects for secular purposes were also made. Production ceased as abruptly as it had started after about one hundred years. No one knows why.

Agriculture began to flourish at about the time of Christ — again without any noticeable transition — and in an area where annual rainfall rarely exceeds a hundred millimetres (by comparison, the annual average for London is 600 mm, New York is 1100 mm). It only rains in the winter months between October and March. For a short time the desert turns into a blooming landscape until the arrival of the dry period in the summer, in which temperatures during the day reach an average 35 C, which causes everything to wither again. No plants can grow during this period without artificial irrigation. The Negev is not a land where the gifts of nature exist in abundance, 'flowing with milk and honey' (Exod.3:8), as was promised by the god Yahweh to the Jewish people. Everything which the desert gives must be hard won. The large size of the wine presses which can still be seen in the ruins of several Nabatean cities today, means that they must have possessed vineyards which extended over several hundred hectares. In this context it is easy to understand why at a later time, when the Negev had become first a Roman and then a Byzantine province, this land was called *Palaestina Salutaris* — blessed Palestine.

The expert way in which the Nabateans made use of the scarce resource of water provides evidence not only of their highly developed agricultural skills; it also requires a skill in social interaction which demands a high degree of societal discipline. Whereas Judea threatened to collapse after being conquered by the Romans after its long and bloody resistance, the Negev flowered both in terms of its agriculture and society. The spread of Christianity probably made a further contribution which helped this region to acquire the *Salutaris* epithet. The arrival of the Romans, which drenched the northern parts of the Holy Land in blood, took place completely peaceably as far as the Nabateans were concerned. In AD 106, the Nabatean kingdom renounced its state sovereignty without any evidence of resistance and became a Roman province. There must have been an awareness among all Nabateans, from the rulers to the ordinary people, that resistance against Rome would bring no benefits, and that their own

Figure 2 (overleaf). Negev landscape near Avdat.   21

existence would be put at risk — as had been shown by the example of Judea. It is true that Nabatea, once so great and mighty, was now split into several provinces, but at the same time it experienced a mighty cultural and economic boost. The renunciation of state and territorial independence was synonymous with a decision in favour of its own cultural development, which received new impulses through Roman influences and the associated opening to the outside world.

The rediscovery of the Nabateans

From the end of the sixteenth century, Palestine as well as the Negev and the southern Jordanian desert became part of the Ottoman Empire. This only changed in 1917, when British troops put an end to Turkish rule. In the preceding centuries, the region had turned into a kind of no man's land. The thinly populated desert region of the Negev in particular, at the outer limit of their territory, was of little importance to its Turkish rulers. No significant income from taxes could be expected from a population which consisted merely of a few Bedouin. Furthermore, it was mainly warlike tribes who lived here and who resisted any attempt by Turkish provincial officials to exercise their power.

It was only in the Europe of the early nineteenth century that a renewed interest in this region awoke for the first time since the end of the Crusades, in the wave of romantic enthusiasm for distant countries, and in particular for the holy places of Christianity. Unconcerned by the dangers which were still posed by such journeys at the time, from the eighteenth century European explorers, but also the plain curious and simply adventurous, set out to reacquaint themselves with the Holy Land. This time, however, not with the sword of the Crusaders but with the resources of the modern scientific mind. It was a new awareness which moved these people to uncover the traces of the past in the search for the origin of their own culture and religion. It is to them that we owe the first modern descriptions of the region, its natural resources and the peoples who are at home there.

Nevertheless, there were few among them who ventured into the Negev. Its inhabitants were as inhospitable towards travellers as they had been towards the Turkish rulers. One of the first to undertake the venture of such an expedition was the German, Ulrich Jasper Seetzen. He had studied natural history and medicine in Göttingen and later ran his own cloth manufacturing business before going exploring in the Orient and Africa. In 1802, at the age of thirty-five, he travelled from Constantinople to Syria and Palestine, acquired the necessary language skills and converted to Islam. By these means he hoped to equip himself to penetrate further into those areas which had so far not been touched by European civilization. In 1805, he reached the areas east of the Jordan disguised in Arab clothing as *Musa al-Hakîm* (Moses the doctor). In the spring of 1806, he visited the Negev. He was one of the first Europeans to have described Mampsis, Avdat and Beersheba. Later he travelled to Mecca at the head of a caravan heavily loaded with archeological finds. Whether it was the greed of the Bedouin which cost him his life in Yemen in 1811, or the attempt by the indigenous population to protect its historical treasures from prying Western eyes will never be known. His writings were only published forty years after his death, which is why he never acquired the fame which he actually deserved as the first European in modern times to have penetrated into these areas.

We owe the rediscovery of Petra, the former Nabatea capital, to Johann Ludwig Burckhardt (1784–1817) from Basle. After completing his studies in England, he offered his services to the African Association, whose purpose was the discovery of as yet unknown areas of the African continent. He disguised himself as a native in order to keep the scientific purpose of his journey a secret. Starting from Syria, where he had acquired some Arabic, he travelled southwards in the direction of Africa in 1812 dressed as a poor pilgrim who called himself 'Sheik Ibrahim.' Burckhardt died in Cairo before he reached the actual goal of his journey, the interior of Africa.

Alois Musil, born in Bohemia in 1868, travelled through the Sinai, the south of Jordan and the Negev at the turn of the century. He too spoke Arabic fluently and in his Arab clothing was taken for a doctor

Figure 3 (overleaf). The mountain village of Sela near Petra. This may have been the place of refuge of the Nabateans mentioned by Diodorus.

and camel merchant. His encounters with the Bedouin of the region several times put him in situations where his life was in danger. When Musil was caught in fighting between hostile Bedouin tribes, he was taken prisoner and only regained his freedom through the intervention of his Arab companions. Four volumes of his travel writings were later published under the title *Arabia Petraea* (Arabia of Stone). The second volume, *Edom,*[1] contains detailed descriptions of Nessana, Mampsis (Kurnub) and Shivta. In 1920, he was given the Chair of Oriental Studies at Prague University.

Another scientist should be included on the list of those who have attempted to decipher the secrets of the former desert population of the Negev; while he is famous for his exploits as Lawrence of Arabia, it is little-known today that shortly before the First World War two young archeologists, T.E. Lawrence and C.L. Woolley, were commissioned by the (British) Palestine Exploration Fund to map the Negev and its archeological sites. (The maps drawn up during this expedition later became an indispensable aid during the capture of the country.) Apart from his military role, Lawrence's greater achievement consisted of his identification of Byzantine and Nabatean ruins in the Negev. Together with Woolley, he documented and photographed some of them and also drew up the first plan of the city of Shivta.

The limits of traditional exploration

Although there has been a considerable growth in archeological re-search in Israel since 1948, researchers primarily directed their atten-tion to the north of the country, whose history reached further into the past. However, the ruins which explorers and travellers had discovered since the start of the nineteenth century in the exploration of the Negev — the former kingdom of the Nabateans — originated from a later period. Strangely, many a researcher whose main love was the Old Testament period, did not extend their research further forwards than the time of Christ, and yet the ruins of Christian churches found in Nabatean settlements in the Negev were built as late as the fourth, fifth and sixth centuries AD. Their investigation therefore appears of lesser importance. In so far as people bothered about the Nabateans at all, they only produced a few and often contradictory results. Current knowledge about the Nabateans often appears so fragmented and with so many gaps that there is still no cohesive picture of their civilization.

Today, it is due particularly to Avraham Negev that there is an awareness of Nabatean culture and its importance. In recent decades, he has been responsible for the most thorough research and teaching in this field. He spent his youth in an agricultural settlement founded in 1943, which was only a few miles from the ruins of the Nabatean city of Elusa (Hebrew: Khaluza). Later, after a serious war wound, he studied archeology. In 1979, excavations took place in Elusa under his supervision which uncovered the largest church in the whole area, as well as a Nabatean theatre. Mampsis and Avdat were also excavated by him.

Geologists, geographers, botanists, zoologists, as well as settlers who moved to the Negev to farm and cultivate the desert, have repeatedly encountered traces from the past in their work. Yet archeological research in desert areas, and the logistics of an expedition, are still accompanied by considerable problems despite modern technology. Difficulties with the water supply, the absence of passable roads and climatic conditions make such an undertaking extraordinarily difficult. Excavation can take place only during short periods of the year when the summer heat, or the risk associated with unpredictable winter flooding, do not endanger excavation work. Then there is the added difficulty that the former Nabatean empire is today divided by the border between Jordan and Israel. Petra, the former capital and stronghold of Nabatean civilization, lies on the Jordanian side, and was inaccessible to Israeli citizens until recently. For decades, this prevented any meeting between researchers from both sides of the border. Even Avraham Negev, who made the investigation of the Nabateans his life's work, and who can look back on forty years of scientific work in this field, only visited Petra for the first time as late as 1995, after the peace agreement.

The history of the Nabateans took a variable course. Its consecutive phases are so different from one another that some researchers even doubt whether one can talk of one and the same people when referring to the settlers in this region in the period from the fifth century BC to the Islamic invasion in 638. Another phenomenon which drives researchers to despair or causes them considerable surprise is the absence of any transitional phases from one cultural stage to the next. The development of Nabatean civilization does not take place as a continuous process but as a series of disjointed changes without any noticeable transition. The characteristics of each phase appear to have reached their highest point of development from the beginning. Architecture, art and religion cannot disguise a certain affinity with the cultures of neighbouring peoples, yet they always display their own particular Nabatean style. Often elements of distant civilizations can be found in Nabatean culture whose existence cannot be satisfactorily explained by reference to the synchronicity which results from the lively cultural exchange between peoples.

In this connection Avraham Negev speaks of 'Nabatean anomalies,' of the ability to absorb new cultural impulses and to use them without long preparatory periods.[2] The Nabateans are unique in this respect. Many attempts have been made to solve the riddle of these strange phenomena of Nabatean history. While in Judea, the land of the scribes, contemporary documents illuminate historical events, this is not the case in Nabatea. Nothing has been found to date which could prove an independent Nabatean record of history. With the exception of the papyri of Nessana, which date from as late as the seventh and eighth Christian centuries, such written records of the Nabateans as exist are to be found in foreign, mostly Greek sources. Yet it may be assumed that the Nabateans had achieved a higher cultural level than other peoples of the region. Inscriptions with everyday messages which have been found on rocks in the desert provide grounds for such an assumption. These inscriptions were made by shepherds who could write. Literacy was not as widespread among other peoples.

Since researchers have no authentic written documents from the Nabateans on which they could base their research, they have to make use of *material* finds, of artifacts and objects of art. Pottery, sculpture and architecture are the stones of a mosaic which are used to reconstruct the picture of a culture which ceased to exist more than a thou-

Figure 4. Wadi near Beersheba.

sand years ago. The results of such a method, of reassembling existing ruins and filling in what is missing, are intended to lead to an understanding of the Nabateans. However, instead of supplying
answers, it is precisely the material remains of the Nabateans which
pose new questions related to the spiritual dimension of their culture
which must therefore remain unanswered.

In order to understand the spiritual side of a civilization, we must
look beyond the population of the region concerned to the external
political, economic and social conditions. Historically, the region of
the Holy Land plays a central part, being the background of the birth
of Christ and Christianity which grew into the greatest religious

influence of today. The proximity of Nabatean civilization to these events, challenges us to understand their role despite their mysterious nature. They were people strongly connected to the world of life forces. Christianity, newly arisen, can, as *re-ligio,* be understood literally as the re-establishment of the connection between human beings and their divine origins. The principle of the resurrection, the conquest of the forces of death, is a central event in this respect which also runs like a leitmotif through Nabatean culture. Was there, in addition to the economic and political reasons for the flowering of their civilization, something like a spiritual mission which gave them a particular historical role at a specific moment in the history of the world of antiquity?

The following attempt to look at the history of the Nabateans and to investigate the significance of the Nabateans in the development of early Christianity, does not, of course, lay any claim to completeness. But perhaps it can pose new questions which might influence or even change the direction of academic research.

CHAPTER TWO

Shepherds, Kings and the Cross: Stages in the Development of a People

The Nabateans emerged from the obscurity of the past into the light of classical history at a time when their culture was already in full flower. The oldest existing writings in which they are mentioned originate at the end of the fourth century BC. It is certain, however, that the first Nabatean tribes were living in that region of north-western Arabia before that time, and many traces of their presence can still be found there. Whereas the historians of the West took a relatively long time to take note of them, there are vague references to their existence in older writings of neighbouring peoples. A list of punished tribes which were conquered by Assurbanipal (668–627 BC) allows us to assume that there were links between the *nabayti* or *nabatu* and the Assyrians at the time of the Assyrian kings in the eighth and seventh centuries BC.

The question as to the exact geographical origins of the Nabatean tribes is still the subject of debate and specialists give various answers. Completely contradictory views have developed. One theory considers the Nabateans to be the descendants of Persian immigrants. Others look for their origins in the Negev, west of Wadi Araba, where they later coalesced into a people.[1]

All of these theories, each of which certainly contains an element of historical truth, relate exclusively to the material finds which have already been mentioned. If we pursue this approach into the past, as set out by a purely archeological way of looking at things, the traces of the Nabateans are lost in the mists of time beyond a certain point. However, the study of the spiritual aspects of Nabatean culture leads to further results. It is not only the material evidence, but also their cast of mind — even if it is found only in fragmentary and poorly preserved form — which can suggest a continuous and cohesive history. If we take the mythological awareness of the Nabateans as a leitmotif, as well as its transformation over the course of more than one thousand years of their cultural development, some light can be thrown into the darkness.

Evidence from the Old Testament

The inhabitants of the Middle East, both Arabs and Jews, considered Abraham to be their common ancestor, just as they do today. The product of a nomad family, Abraham moved from Mesopotamia to the land of Canaan as God commanded him, and settled there. But his journey began by leading him through what was to become the territory of the Nabateans. 'Then the Lord appeared to Abraham, and said, "To your descendants I will give this land." ... And Abraham journeyed on, still going toward the Negeb.' (Gen.12:7–9)

Plagued by hunger, Abraham first of all journeyed to Egypt before he returned to the promised land on the instructions of God. He was already at an advanced age and still without children when the sacrificial covenant with the god Yahweh was entered into (Gen.15). In 'a dread and great darkness' the future of his descendants was revealed to him, who were not to find peace for a very long time. Up to that time Sarah, his wife, had not born him any children. That is why she gave him Hagar, his maid, to be his wife. She became pregnant but treated Sarah with such disdain that she was cast out by Abraham and had to flee into the desert. There she met an angel:

> The angel of the Lord also said to her, I will so greatly
> multiply your descendants that they cannot be numbered for

multitude. And the angel of the Lord said to her, Behold, you are with child, and shall bear a son; you shall call his name Ishmael; because the Lord has given heed to your affliction. He shall be a wild ass of a man ... And Hagar bore Abraham a son: and Abraham called the name of his son, which Hagar bore, Ishmael. (Gen.16:10–15)

Ishmael is traditionally considered to be the father of all the Arab tribes. Like Jacob, he had twelve sons. However, unlike the twelve tribes of the ancient Hebrew people they did not remain united as a single people but each developed into an individual ethnic group:

These are the descendants of Ishmael, Abraham's son, whom Hagar the Egyptian, Sarah's maid, bore to Abraham. These are the names of the sons of Ishmael named in order of their birth: Nebaioth, the firstborn of Ishmael, and Kedar, Adbeel, Mibsam, Mishma, Dumah, Massa, Hadar, Tema, Jetur, Naphish, and Kedemah. These are the sons of Ishmael and these are their names, by their villages and by their encampments; twelve princes according to their tribes. (Gen.25:12–16).

The tradition that the Arab peoples descended from the line of Ishmael, and in particular from the line of the firstborn Nebaioth, appears to have been known also to Flavius Josephus, who was the descendant of a Judean priestly family, and took part in the revolt against the Romans in Galilee in 66 AD as one of its leaders. In his writings, he mentions the Nabateans as powerful, hitherto unconquered neighbours of the province of Judea.[2]

Unfortunately, there is little information in the Old Testament about what happened to the descendants of Ishmael:

Abraham took another wife, whose name was Keturah. She bore him Zimran, Jokshan, Medan, Midian, Ishbak, and Shuah. Jokashan was the father of Saba, and Dedan ... Abraham gave all he had to Isaac. But to the sons of his

concubines, Abraham gave gifts, and while he was still living
he sent them away from his son Isaac, eastward to the east
country. (Gen.25:1–6).

Various related concepts can be traced back to the Hebrew conso-
nant root 'A-R-B (the B can be 'soft,' becoming V). The designation
Arab or *Arabic* which has its origins in those three consonants can
therefore also be interpreted in various ways depending on their context. *'erev* means evening, *ma'arav* the West, the direction from
which the wind blows at evening twilight. But *'erev* can also mean
mixture, particularly in an ethnic sense. Thus in Exodus (12:38): 'A
mixed multitude also went up with them, and very many cattle, both
flocks and herds.' *'Erev-rav,* which has the same root as *Arab* and is
translated here as 'mixed multitude,' indicates a mixture of people of
various ethnic backgrounds. They travel for a while with the sons of
Israel through the Sinai desert.

From the point of view of the authors of the Old Testament, the
neighbours in the south-east were therefore a 'mixture of peoples' descended from the sons of Ishmael, and thus *Arabs.* They are described
as herders and inhabitants of the desert, which is also evident from a
prophecy of Jeremiah (3:2): 'like an Arab in the wilderness.' They
came from the east, from *the Orient,* to the borders of the fertile land
and to the coast of the sea into which the sun sinks at night. In another
mention in the Old Testament from the time of the kingdom of Judea,
the Arabs appear as wealthy animal breeders and owners of large
herds:

> And the fear of the Lord fell upon all the kingdoms of the
> lands that were round about Judah, and they made no war
> against Jehoshaphat. Some of the Philistines brought
> Jehoshaphat presents, and silver for tribute; and the Arabs also
> brought him seven thousand seven hundred rams, and seven
> thousand seven hundred he-goats. (2Chron.17:10f).

In Jeremiah we find a further interesting statement which relates to
the descendants of the Rechabites. These are held in high regard by

Jeremiah, because they have remained true to an ancient oath which they made jointly as a tribal community:

> But they answered, 'We will drink no wine, for Jonadab the son of Rechab, our father, commanded us, "You shall not drink wine, neither you, nor your sons for ever; you shall not build a house; you shall not sow seed; you shall not plant or have a vineyard; but you shall live in tents all your days, that you may live many days in the land where you sojourn".' (Jer.35:6f)

In terms of its content, this characterization is in complete agreement with a description of the Nabateans by Diodorus, which was written four hundred years later.

Saba: original home of the Nabateans?

The kingdom of Saba can be shown to have existed as early as the eleventh century BC in the south of the Arabian peninsula in what today is Yemen.[3] In classical times, this region was largely cut off from the Egyptian and Mesopotamian centres of civilization by extensive desert areas, and could only be reached after exhausting journeys along the caravan routes, which often took months. Contact between the western world and the southern part of Arabia — in particular the kingdom of Saba — was largely established through the trade in valuables from this region, such as myrrh and incense as well as gold. These had to be transported through the desert over a distance of more than three thousand kilometres before they reached the Mediterranean ports from where they were shipped to the western world. Saba appears to have been the only southern Arabian country which was known beyond its frontiers through its trade.

Archeological findings indicate that there was continuous settlement in Saba from, at the latest, the eleventh century BC onwards. This is also the time in which its civilization flowered, reaching its climax in the eighth and seventh centuries BC. The rulers of Saba were priest-kings, called *Mukharib,* whose power was based on cultic and religious authority. More than ten thousand deciphered writings and numerous excavations over the last century have thrown some light on the history of Saba. The population was partly settled and partly nomadic and possessed a highly developed system of agriculture and an ingenious water supply system. Despite its desert climate, Saba had sufficient water reserves and had therefore developed agriculture from very ancient times onwards. Dams were built and the water was guided to the arable areas by artificial canals. This irrigation system was unique in the classical world. There was a special awareness and know-how in the civilization of Saba which achieved a high degree of fertility in desert areas.

The people of Saba were the guardians of sun mysteries, whose symbol became the sun carried in the vessel of the moon. The moon was the symbol of the natural forces which were effective during the period of darkness. At the same time, it was also a symbol of fertility, and the constant, never-ending renewal of life in nature. It dies after each cycle in order to be reborn. The sun, on the other hand, was considered to be an expression of the everlasting, life-giving principle. In the desert it was at its most intense. It is therefore no great surprise that a civilization which arose in the desert should have a particularly intense relationship with the sun, and that the divine beings hidden behind its visible form were experienced in a different way by the desert inhabitants. Despite its destructive power, which could turn everything to ash, it was considered to be the giver of life. The image of the phoenix rising from ashes is a consistently recurring motif in the civilization of Saba and at the same time a leitmotif of the mythological awareness which, based on the geographical and climatic conditions, had developed an understanding of the secrets of death and resurrection.

Gold, incense and myrrh were among the most important goods which were taken by the Nabateans from far distant Saba in the south of the Arabian peninsula to the Mediterranean coast. The desert presented no obstacle to its inhabitants. They led their caravans to the boundary of the territory occupied by the Mediterranean peoples, quickly to disappear again into the uncharted expanses of the desert. The Nabateans had an excellent reputation in classical antiquity not least because of their animal husbandry. In addition, they were held in high esteem for their masterly handling of the most valuable substance of the desert — water — which was vital for life. The story is told of King Uzziah, a contemporary of Isaiah, whom God helped against the Philistines and the Arabs (2Chron.26:7). And then — as if Uzziah had received new impulses and a spiritual interchange from these peoples — the story continues:

> And he built towers in the desert and hewed out many cisterns,
> for he had large herds, both in the Shephehah and in the plain,
> and he had farmers and vine dressers in the hills and in the
> fertile lands, for he loved the soil. (2Chron.26:10).

Love of the earth, the ability to handle the life-giving element of water, to tame it with the human hand, are characteristics which already determined life in the kingdom of Saba at this time. It therefore appears justified to search for the roots of the Nabateans there, as the other characteristics of their civilization coincide with those of the civilization of Saba both in time and in character. The Bible provides a great deal of help in this respect. It contains contemporary information which provides a true picture of the situation at that time.

However, it cannot be deduced from any of these texts that the Nabateans were the product of the *mixture* of the descendants of Nebaioth and the inhabitants of Saba, and cannot, therefore, be claimed with absolute certainty. Only once in the Bible, namely in the prophecies of Isaiah, are the descendants of both these tribes mentioned in the same context. Isaiah is describing the period after the coming of the Messiah. His visions display similarities with the type of spiritual vision which was to be experienced by Paul several centuries later at the gates of Damascus. Isaiah also names the first peoples who would gather round the new spiritual light:

> Arise, shine; for your light has come, and the glory of the Lord
> has risen upon you. For, behold, the darkness shall cover the
> earth, and thick darkness the peoples: but the Lord will arise
> upon you, and his glory will be seen upon you. And nations
> shall come to your light, and kings to the brightness of your
> rising ... Then you shall see, and be radiant, and your heart

shall thrill and rejoice; because the abundance of the sea shall be turned to you, the wealth of the nations shall come to you ... All those from Saba shall come: they shall bring gold and frankincense; and shall proclaim the praise of the Lord. All the flocks of Kedar shall be gathered together to you, the rams of Nebaioth shall minister to you. (Isa.60:1–7).

Although the book of Isaiah is a very old document which may have originated in the seventh century BC, it does not contain the only Old Testament account from this time, which describes features characteristic of the Nabateans; features which were described in later writings of Greek origin after 312 BC. In Isaiah's prophecies, the sons of the Nebaioth and Saba are characterized in a way which appears to correspond with the tribes which were later given the name *Nabateans.* Isaiah reports the coming of the saviour, the Messiah. The predictions of the prophet are usually related only to the ancient Hebrews. But we will see later that it was precisely the Nabateans who would fulfil Isaiah's prophecies. They came from Saba, brought gold and incense and were among the first peoples who, as one, declared their faith in Christianity.

The people of Saba, too, were Arabs who considered themselves to be the descendants of Abraham. Their earliest mention as a people is connected with the construction of Solomon's temple in Jerusalem.

Now when the Queen of Sheba heard of the fame of Solomon concerning the name of the Lord, she came to test him with hard questions. She came to Jerusalem with a very great train, with camels that bear spices, and very much gold, and precious stones: and when she came to Solomon, she told him all that was on her mind. (1 Kings 10:1f).

According to the Old Testament, this meeting between the two representatives of different civilizations is characterized by serious trials, but also by mutual recognition of, and respect for, each other's spiritual and material wealth. This meeting was also the starting point for a lively trade in the riches of the Orient (1 Kings 10:10), including

40

substances for ritual purposes which had hitherto been unknown in Solomon's kingdom: incense, myrrh, and gold. The holy writings of the other religions originating in this region also described the Queen of Sheba as an outstanding personality characterized by a spirituality of a very specific nature which she sought to impart to her people. In the gospel of St Luke, Jesus refers to the Queen of Sheba as helping him in judgement on Judgement Day: 'For as Jonas became a sign to men of the Ninevites, so will the Son of Man be to this generation. The queen of the south will arise in the judgment with the men of this generation, and condemn them.' (Luke 11:30f).

In Jewish sources the Queen of Sheba often appears as a demonic figure.[4] Much of the original knowledge of the Judeans about the common spiritual roots of both civilizations was lost with the destruction of the Temple in Jerusalem. The strict isolation of their own spiritual wealth from outside influences was an attempt to prevent the subversion of Jewish culture and its traditional beliefs. There are only a few remnants of such knowledge in Jewish sources from this time. Thus the story is told in connection with the preparation of the royal visit from Saba to Jerusalem, that the Queen was a priestess of the sun god and that the ravens which King Solomon had sent her had blocked her view of the horizon during the ritual. A later King of Saba bore the name *Abd Shams* — 'servant of the sun.'[5]

The Koran, too, contains a clear indication that the Queen of Sheba had the reputation of being a sun worshipper as late as the seventh century AD. The hoopoe with its sun-like plumage, sent by King Solomon as his ambassador, returned and reported:

I see what you do not see, and I bring you tidings from Saba. See, I found a woman ruling the country, who possessed all things, and she had a magnificent throne. And I found her and her people worshipping the sun ... (27:22–24).

The settlement of the Negev by the tribes of Saba

At the time under discussion, the empire ruled by Solomon stretched to the Israelite port of Ezion Geber on the Red Sea. Jerusalem was conquered by the Babylonians in 586 BC and the Temple of Solomon was destroyed. The difficult years in Babylonian exile began for the Jewish people. The links between Jerusalem and Saba survived the confusion of this time both on a religious and trading level and were maintained by experienced merchants and seafarers who journeyed through the desert with their caravans and sailed along the Red Sea coast to the ports of Saba. Their journeys would take months. Bases were established along the most heavily travelled routes over many generations, particularly near oases, with resting places for travellers, religious sites and burial places for those who died along the way.

After the destruction of Jerusalem Judea and the Negev in particular became a kind of no man's land. Although people came from Babylon to Samaria, who were to become the Samaritans, that whole stretch of land remained as if abandoned. Thus it may be assumed that those who had been at home in the desert for a long time and knew how to survive in it continued to live their usual life and continued to trade undisturbed.

While the kingdom of Saba in the south of the Arabian peninsula had already begun to decline at this time, the Babylonian rulers of Palestine would have been the source of numerous economic and cultural impulses which may have attracted many people. From trading, the inhabitants of Saba knew the northern desert regions. They are likely to have also been attracted by spiritual kinship with Babylonian culture, thinking, which led to their increased presence in the desert areas of the Negev. A new civilization arose here based on a major tradition stretching back a long way. Increasing numbers of Sabean tribes penetrated the territory bringing their culture and their beliefs with them.

Directly north-west of Petra, the Nabatean 'Jerusalem,' there is a small but significant archeological site called Tawilan. This place lies above the entrance to the *Siq,* the gorge which forms the natural corridor by which Petra is entered. There had been settlers in Tawilan towards the end of the eighth century BC, that is in the time in which the first Sabeo-Nabatean tribes are thought to have been in the area. Large amounts of painted pottery from the sixth century BC were found there and indicate early settlement of the site. The imprint of a Sabean seal has also been found there. It shows an altar with the crescent moon suspended above it carrying the disc of the sun. This is a typical symbol for the sun mysteries of Saba. It is one of the few pieces of evidence indicating the presence of dignitaries from Saba (for only they would have been in possession of such a seal) at such an early time.

Like the Judeans, the Nabateans lived in a type of messianic expectation. Filled with the wisdom of the ancient sun mysteries, the descendants of the inhabitants of Saba retained a knowledge of the universal significance of the approach of the sun-being in the human incarnation of Christ. Starting from the prophecies that were revealed to the tribes of Saba, it is not at all unlikely that they also sought geographical proximity to the expected events, and that the tribes began to migrate to the desert country in the north abandoned by the Israelites, where a political vacuum had been created. This was the beginning of a gradual process of settlement. Increasing numbers of people abandoned their nomadic lifestyle, creating the conditions leading to state structures and the establishment of a kingdom.

Records of the Nabateans in classical history

The first recorded contact between the desert population of the Negev and Greco-European civilization did not occur until Alexander the Great penetrated the Judean cultural area. According to the historian, Diodorus, around 332 BC, the High Priest in Jerusalem opened the city gates and without battle surrendered with his people to the conquering Macedonian army led by Alexander,[6] but the Greek conquest of Judea hardly affected the life of the population. Alexander carried on along the Mediterranean coast towards Egypt. The desert south-east of Judea remained almost untouched by Alexander's campaign. Yet it was at this first, if brief, meeting of the Orient with European civilization when we first hear of the Nabateans in a new type of historical writing, specifically aimed at subsequent generations, in that it not only wrote down and recorded dates and facts, but also *described* historical processes in their context. To this day it is unclear whether the Nabateans had any sort of comparable historical documentation.

Diodorus Siculus, the Greek historian of the first century BC, mentions the Nabateans in two different places in his work. The first time is in his description of Asia and then again when he describes the military campaign of Antigonus Monophthalmos, the *one-eyed*. Antigonus was one of the rivals for the succession of Alexander the Great who came up against the resistance of the Nabateans in his attempt to extend the borders of the empire. Diodorus, whose work contains much valuable information about the nature of the Arab tribes, their lifestyle and customs, quotes a description from 312 BC in this context. Its author was Hieronymous of Cardia, who was governor of the Dead Sea region: 'This country lies between Syria and Egypt. It is divided among many different peoples. The eastern region of this country is inhabited by Arabs called Nabateans.'[7]

Hieronymous had been instructed by Antigonus to capture the asphalt trade on the Dead Sea which was controlled by the Nabateans. He did not achieve his aim but he left us the oldest reliable report about the Nabateans in this region. This says quite clearly: the Nabateans are *Arabs*!

The Semitic root of the word, N-B-T, from which the term Nabateans is derived, means *germinate, sprout* — a process which takes place in the plant world and which starts with the contact between seeds and water. In a further derivation it also means 'those who dig for water.' The Nabateans had succeeded in a wonderful way in doing justice to their name as a people or tribe. Diodorus' Asia report, which we have already mentioned, contains interesting details in this respect, too, about the theatre of Nabatean history:

The Arabs, who are called Nabateans, live in a strip of land which is partly desert, partly without water although a small part of it is fertile. They rob and pillage neighbouring countries. In war they are difficult to subdue for they have built cisterns at regular intervals in this waterless zone, the knowledge of which they keep strictly secret. So they withdraw into this country and are protected from all danger. They alone know where the hidden water is to be found and therefore have sufficient water at their disposal. Those who try to pursue them die from lack of water or return to their countries after much suffering. That is how the Nabateans manage to keep their freedom ... No enemy has been able to vanquish them, however many and powerful armies he has sent against them.[8]

According to Diodorus' report, Antigonus, the one-eyed, succeeded in conquering Syria and Phoenicia without a fight. He thought that he would be able to repeat these military successes in the conquest of the Nabateans and ordered his companion, Athenaios, to invade their country at the head of a speedy cavalry and four thousand troops in order to capture as much of their treasure as possible. But this campaign failed. After some success in conquering one of the Nabatean fortresses and slaughtering the women and children left behind there, the Nabatean warriors counter-attacked and destroyed the Macedonian army. Afterwards, the reports say, the Nabateans sent a message to Antigonus in which they blamed Athenaios' lack of skill for the defeat of the Greek troops. An extraordinarily rare gesture under the prevailing circumstances: a victory over the forces of a world power was not ascribed to one's own superiority and celebrated as a glorious feat of one's own nation, but was seen as a weakness of the opponent. The impact of that defeat appears to have persuaded Antigonus to abandon his desire to conquer the territory under the control of the Nabateans and he cultivated friendly relations with them. He did, nevertheless, later decide on another attempt to conquer them. He placed his son Demetrios at the head of four thousand horsemen and four thousand foot soldiers.

For three days this army marched through the trackless desert yet the Nabatean scouts did not miss them when they invaded their country. Diodorus writes about the fire signals flashing from mountain to mountain to warn the population of the Greek invasion, about *Sela,* the 'rock' on which the women and children found refuge, about the herds which were hidden in the desert as well as about the attack on Sela which was beaten back in the course of a single day. The next morning, Demetrios approached this place again. One of the 'barbarians' turned to Demetrios and called to him:

> King Demetrios, which desire or purpose leads you to fight us? We live in the desert where there is neither water nor grain nor wine nor anything else which could be of use to you. We do not want to live as slaves and have therefore chosen to live in the desert, in a country where there is a shortage of everything which other peoples prize. We have decided to live like the beasts in the field and cause you no harm. Therefore we appeal to you and your father to leave us unharmed and, in return for presents which we want to give you, withdraw your troops and in future consider the Nabateans as friends. For even if you wanted to, you could not stay more than a few days in this country for you have no water and no provisions and cannot force us to lead a different life. All you will have are a few rebellious slaves who cannot change the way they live.[9]

Demetrios was given lavish presents and an escort out of the desert. In the subsequent period we only know of one other attempt by the Greeks to bring the territory of the Nabateans under their control. Hieronymous, whose writings are quoted by Diodorus, wanted to stop the Nabateans from collecting the asphalt which periodically rises to the surface of the Dead Sea. But a counter-offensive by the Nabateans in reed boats also made this attack fail. Here we must wonder at the unique attitude of the Nabateans to choose no other landscape than the desert as the place of their existence despite the riches which they acquired.

Diodorus also tells us about some customs and habits of the Nabateans which they were convinced guaranteed them their freedom and thus had to be strictly followed. Their home was the desert in which there were no rivers and few springs. They did not build houses, they did not plant trees and they drank no wine. Anyone who ignored these rules could be punished by death. Hieronymous explained these strict principles as protecting this people or tribe from outside influences and thus preserving its independence. But such rules of behaviour cannot be seen only from a societal perspective. They are also based on religious conviction.

The Old Testament reports that the Prophet Jeremiah was sent by God to the house of the Rechabites in order to tempt them into drinking wine (Jer.35:6f). But they resisted the temptation (see p. 37). This adherence to the ancient rules is praised by God as an example of true piety. Centuries later, these same qualities were described by Diodorus as the basic characteristics of Nabatean civilization:

> Some of the Nabateans breed camels, others breed sheep which graze in the desert. The Nabateans are the wealthiest among all the Arab shepherd tribes, even if they number no more than ten thousand. Many of them bring expensive spices, myrrh and incense from *Arabia eudaemon* [Saba] to the coast. They are extremely freedom-loving; when an enemy nears, they find refuge in the desert which offers them protection. For the desert is without water and inaccessible to anyone else. They dig subterranean, lined cisterns and that is why the desert offers only them protection. In some places the earth is soft and clay-like, in others it consists of soft stone. They dig large caves whose mouths they keep very small and unobtrusive but which expand as they go downwards until they are so large at the base that each side is a hundred feet long. They are filled with rain water and they stop the entrance in such a way that it is on a level with the surrounding ground. But they leave signs behind which only they know. Others cannot see them. They water their herds every third day so that they do not constantly need water in waterless regions and if they have to flee. Their food consists of milk and meat and they also use plants which grow wild there as food. For pepper grows where they live and there is much 'tree honey' on the trees which they drink mixed with water.[10]

This oldest description of the Nabatean way of life which has been preserved paints the picture of a civilization which has perfected the nomadic lifestyle, which is protected by an orally transmitted code of behaviour and which only associates itself in a very limited way with all the things which a civilization produces by way of material goods. The stone walls which divide human beings from the outside world did not as yet exist, merely a thin tent canopy made of camel hair. Life in tents did not tie people to fixed places. They could respond to the climatic conditions and move their herds to the best grazing, but this specific lifestyle affected not only the kind of housing, but also all household tools. All vessels were, as far as possible, made of unbreakable material. Earthenware containers were not particularly practical for these desert inhabitants in a nomadic age. They could not be folded, were heavy and broke easily. The sowing of wheat or barley, types of grain which can grow in certain regions of the Negev under favourable conditions, would have required the Nabateans to return to a particular place at a specific time for the harvest. Orchards and vineyards would have needed constant care and permanent settlement.

There was only a single fortified place of refuge: *Sela* the *rock* mentioned by Diodorus which provided protection at times of danger. It is no longer possible to determine today where exactly it lay, whether it was close to Petra or on the western bank of Wadi Araba. Petra itself lies hidden in a basin-shaped valley of a rocky mountain range, but although its name means *rock* this does not necessarily refer to the aforementioned place. The city was established as a religious centre of the Nabateans as late as two hundred years after the events described by Diodorus. Traditionally, two rocks near Petra are considered to be possible sites (see Figure 3) which correspond to the description of Hieronymous of Cardia. Avraham Negev considers another possible site south-west of the Dead Sea, north of the Ein Boqeq spring where large amounts of Nabatean pottery was found.[11]

People who knew how to survive in the desert under extreme climatic conditions must have developed a very special relationship with the natural elements. The four elements — earth, air, fire and water — interact in a completely different way in the desert than in a temperate landscape. The mineral element in the earth is fully exposed to the eye and is visible everywhere in various shades of colour. If the few oases dotted throughout the territory are left out of account, water is only visible in winter on the earth's surface. On most days of the year, the sun is fully exposed in a cloudless sky, and during the night the world of the stars speaks to the inhabitants in all its glory. These features of the environment also characterized the nature of the people there, their beliefs, view of the world, knowledge of the forces which are at work behind the natural phenomena, and the particular way in which they handle these forces.

From the following centuries, there are unfortunately no contemporary documents of significance which could provide information about the continued settlement of the Negev and the development of Nabatean culture. In the time which had elapsed since the Nabateans penetrated the Negev, the camel took the place of the donkey as the beast of burden.[12] Before camels were domesticated, long-distance trade by land routes was not very advanced. The expansion of trade was linked to the *invention* of writing and its use in societies which lived in relative isolation in the desert. Trade on a larger scale requires the use of writing. An adult camel could a considerably heavier weights than a donkey, and camel trains through the desert thus became an increasingly lucrative occupation. Trade became one of the most important activities during this time. If previously there were perhaps only a few hundred merchants who crossed the desert and brought goods from the south to the Mediterranean, they now formed a significant part of the total population. The occupation of camel breeder was highly respected in society, but a large part of the population continued with its shepherd existence. According to later accounts, the goats, sheep and cattle bred by the Nabateans, and their products, were highly prized throughout the region.[13]

Over the course of time, the cultural and political focus of world events shifted increasingly from Mesopotamia towards Europe. Both in Mesopotamia and ancient Egypt trade was largely conducted by water; on Mesopotamia's two great rivers and on the Nile. The predominance of the Greeks in the Mediterranean area and the Middle East meant that trade switched more and more to land routes. The demand of the wealthy sections of the population for products which

*Figure 5. Oldest known Nabatean
inscription, approx. 164 BC, Elusa.*

had to be imported from faraway countries was constantly growing.
In this respect the Nabateans assumed a key position, for they were
the only ones who knew the desert well enough to open it up for trade.

The Nabatean kingdom and its special features

The first Nabatean inscription which we know about (Figure 5) is
dated 164 BC, roughly 150 years after Antigonus' unsuccessful campaign. It was discovered in Elusa and it is assumed that it was composed for the consecration of a temple or another holy site: 'This is
the [sanctified?] place built by Natiru, at the time of Aretas, King of
the Nabateans.' Unfortunately, this inscription, like many other finds,
has disappeared, and its whereabouts are unknown. Only a copy by
Jaussen, Savignac and Vincent, three Dominican monks who re-
searched the region in the early twentieth century, has been preserved.[14]

The inscription makes clear that, at the time of the wars of the succession, the Nabateans were engaged in a process which stood in
complete contrast to the development of other peoples in the region.

50

Whereas other groups of peoples had been forced to give up their cultural and independence under Greek occupation, the Nabateans strengthened their independence during this period, resulting in their own state under the rule of their kings.

There is no historical documentation of this process, which concluded with the unification of various clans and tribal groups into a kingdom, which was based on joint interests as well as common religious and spiritual traits. We can only guess how it happened and perhaps imagine it in the following way: inspired by their spiritual leaders, caravan travellers began to settle in the Negev. Family by family, in small groups, they formed colonies in the area. There might have been different reasons why they did this, although economic considerations will certainly have played a major role. The long distances between the tent encampments of the nomads with their constantly changing locations, the lack of water and the short grazing season made it a necessity for the tribes to integrate more closely in order to realize their common existential interests.

However, there was also a spiritual and religious feeling of cohesion which united the various tribes. In the protected and easily defended mountains east of Wadi Araba, Petra quickly developed into a religious centre which was visited by nomads at regular intervals; it finally became the capital of Nabatea in recognition of its importance. A core group of religious leaders had succeeded in binding a loose and ethnically diverse association of tribes more firmly together, and in imposing their authority on a wider group than those who were linked to them by blood. Anyone willing to associate themselves with this civilization on a spiritual level, but also with respect to lifestyle and environment — the desert — could become a *Nabatean.* This created a popular identity which did not have an ethnic foundation in the traditional sense, and was based on a common ideal and not on common descent. In historical terms, all of this happened in a relatively short period of time. All growth processes are accelerated in the desert — including perhaps the growth of a people.

In the classical world, a king was seen primarily as a ruler of a clearly defined territory, but the land of the Nabateans did not have any clear frontiers except with Judea to the north. The apparently end-

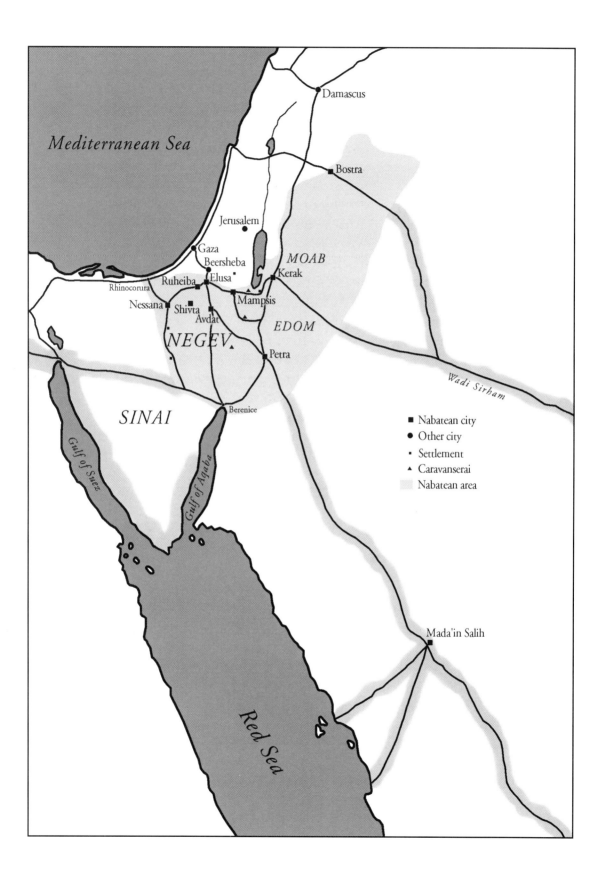

Mediterranean Sea

Damascus

Bostra

Jerusalem

Gaza
Beersheba
MOAB
Ruheiba Elusa Kerak
Rhinocorura
Nessana Mampsis
Shivta
Avdat
EDOM
NEGEV
Petra

Berenice

SINAI

Wadi Sirham

■ Nabatean city
● Other city
· Settlement
▲ Caravanserai
░ Nabatean area

Gulf of Suez

Gulf of Aqaba

Mada'in Salih

Red Sea

less desert which surrounded it, and the crude methods of surveying and cartography of the time, did not permit clear borders to be drawn. In any case, given the sparse population, they would have been meaningless. The further Nabatean influence reached towards the south and the east, the less clear the course of the frontiers became. At the extreme periphery of the kingdom, the Nabateans only controlled the actual roads (Map 1). To the left or right of these routes was a sparsely inhabited no man's land. The opportunities for a king resident in Petra to have any direct influence on what was happening two or three thousand kilometres away from his capital were extremely small. It could be months before a dispatch arrived by caravan in Petra.

King Aretas I, mentioned in the inscription of Elusa, was the first Nabatean *statesman* with a title which allows us to conclude that he ruled over the kingdom in the European sense of the word. It would probably be wrong to imagine the Nabatean king in the mould of rulers who existed among the Greeks. Equally, there were differences from the style of rulership in Judea, where there was a fundamental division between the office of king and priest. Undoubtedly the Nabateans used elements of Greek culture and state craft, but ancient traditions continued at the same time. This was one of the special features about the Nabateans; they linked tried and tested elements with new ones to create something of their own. It is not difficult to imagine that the external face of the kingdom was adapted to its environment despite its Hellenistic influence, but that internally the ancient traditions played a dominant role. The king continued to be a kind of tribal chief. He most likely originated from a line which could trace its descent from the earliest settlers from Saba. Inscriptions found particularly on the Sinai peninsula show that other tribes also settled in the border regions of the kingdom.[15] The number of such tribes who began to consider themselves as Nabateans, for religious, ethnic, cultural, political or economic reasons, grew steadily. This made it imperative for central government to develop.

We know of eleven Nabatean kings. Apart from individual references in the Bible and in the writings of Josephus, it is mainly inscriptions and coins which have contributed to determining the Nabatean succession. The absence of reliable sources and clear

Map 1. Nabatean realms during Hellenistic times (after A. Negev).   53

references has turned the reconstruction of the Nabatean royal dynasty into a puzzle.[16]

c. 168 BC	*Aretas I* (Tyrannos?)
120–96 BC	*Aretas II* (Erotimus)
96–85 BC	*Obodas I* (Avdat)
85–84 BC	*Rabel I* (Rabb'il)
84–62 BC	*Aretas III* (Philhellenos)
62–59 BC	*Obodas II*
59–30 BC	*Malichus I*
30–9 BC	*Obodas III,* accompanied in office by the *Epitropos* Syllaeus
9 BC–40 AD	*Aretas IV* (Philodemos = who loves his people)
40–70 AD	*Malichus II*
70–106 AD	*Rabel II* (Soter = Redeemer, who brings his people life and freedom)

This list is controversial. A reliable identification of kings with the same name poses problems. The addition of Latin numerals is the invention of historians who have taken their guide from western traditions, and the numbers are not found in any documents of the time. The epithets, however, such as *Philodemos* (who loves his people), *Philhellenos* (who loves Hellenic culture), or *Soter* (redeemer), are authentic. Whether the kingship was passed down through families is not known. It does appear, however, that a new ruler liked to assume the name of his predecessor on ascending the throne.

It is not known when Nabatean tribal leaders were given their Greek epithets *Basileos* or *Tyrannos,* and thus the royal title, for the first time, but there are many indications (such as the dating of inscriptions and coins) that it must have happened in the second half of the fourth century BC, at the time of Alexander's campaign. Aretas I is the first Nabatean ruler whom we know by name. The determination of the period of his rule is based on a mention in the Maccabees as well as the lost inscription of Elusa (Figure 5), which was dated by the style of writing to 164 BC.

Altogether, there were only two kings whose time in office lasted less than ten years. Aretas IV, the contemporary of Christ, ruled for forty-eight years and the last of his dynasty, Rabel II, managed thirty-six years. This provides evidence of a very stable form of rulership which appears all the more surprising if we take into consideration that the kings ruled, other than in the Greek and Roman world, by popular approval and were subject to public criticism.

At the beginning of the Nabatean kingdom, at the end of the third and beginning of the second century BC, the king tended to fulfil religious rather than political duties. That is why the office of king was considered to be particularly significant among Nabateans.[17] They were priest-kings, spiritual leaders of their society, in which state institutions played an insignificant role but the community-building forces were all the stronger among the population. This dual function of the ruler also continued the old traditions of Saba. It is one of the peculiarities of the Nabatean system that in a kingdom which arose at such a late stage, and which took on so many features of Hellenistic culture, the ruler maintained his function as a religious leader.

In the final decades of the fourth century BC events in the Middle East were determined by the collapse of the Persian empire, and the premature death of Alexander the Great. The desert regions of the Middle East were largely ignored by the major powers, which were now primarily concerned with internal power struggles. This meant that the Nabatean state was able to develop without outside interference. The Hellenistic influence in the second century BC was so strong that it affected the very form of state, but the different religious consciousness and the mentality of the people produced a set of principles which prevented the total assimilation of external social forms; they were adhered to even during the time of the monarchy. Above all, this included a love of freedom which the desert had bred in the people over a period of centuries. There were, therefore, practically no slaves in the Nabatean kingdom, which other civilizations liked to bring home as war booty. The Nabateans were wealthy enough to be able to pay for the services they required.

As well as their love of freedom, the peaceable nature of the Nabateans was also a determining characteristic of their monarchy.

This governed not only their behaviour towards other peoples, but also their daily life was largely conducted in peace. Strabo reports:

> Athenodoros, a worldly-wise friend of mine, who visited the Petrans, told full of admiration that he had encountered many Romans and other foreigners there. The foreigners sued each other and the local people in court, but he never noticed the local people suing each other in court. All lived in complete peace with one another.[18]

Strabo's report relates to the last third of the first century BC and indicates that, besides the king, a different person held the office of *Epitropos,* which might be translated as *brother, guardian* or *chancellor.* He refers to an *Epitropos* called Syllaeus, who held office alongside King Obodas III and who knew how to use the weaknesses of the king for his own purposes. This is a clear indication that the king was concerned with social and religious affairs while foreign policy was the domain of the trustee, the *brother.*

A tremendous amount of building was started in the first century BC. A people which for a long time had rejected stone as a building material now began to create impressive and independent styles of architecture. The first things to be built were the Petran tombs and temples, followed later by superior domestic buildings. At the same time they started to produce high-quality pottery. Widespread horse breeding also developed, but the most surprising thing was the development of agriculture in the desert, like that undertaken eight hundred years earlier in Saba, and which must have originated from there. No other civilization had hitherto succeeded in developing a similar kind of irrigation technology which was capable of turning vast areas of desert into blooming gardens.

The Nabatean kingdom existed for at least two hundred and seventy years. As in all areas of its activity, in architecture, art, even in the depiction of its gods, which changed several times from one generation to the next, it is possible to see clearly Nabatean characteristics in the way that the state was governed, despite the constant enrichment of this civilization by outside influences.

The Christian era

Alexander's campaign did not affect the lives of the Nabateans in any significant way. They succeeded throughout the pre-Christian centuries, in preserving their political and cultural independence. Now the birth of Christ was approaching. The birth of a new world religion began as a concealed event. Historians did not take any notice of what happened in a stable in Jerusalem, culminating in the work of Jesus, his crucifixion and resurrection. Only a few noticed the signs which ushered in the new age, and followed the call to Jerusalem to take part in this key event in the salvation of mankind through Christ turned man.

History shows that Christianity spread rapidly in the Nabatean kingdom. Since the rule of the emperor Trajan, the Negev increasingly lost its importance as a transit route for caravans. Trajan had his own roads built, such as the *Via Traiana Nova,* which moved trade to the eastern side of Wadi Araba (Map 2, p. 128). From this time onwards, large areas of the Negev were turned into agricultural land where the idea of the resurrection, the victory of life over death, took visible form and was thus able to take root in people's consciousness in a vivid way — and did indeed did so.

Little is known about the process of Christianization of the population of the Negev, particularly in the first three centuries. The Nabatean kingdom became a Roman province in 106 AD. After the death of King Rabel II, the Nabateans subjected themselves to the Roman claim to power without resistance. If the Judeans lost their sovereignty in a process marked by bloodshed and national catastrophe, Nabatea came under foreign rule peacefully and without any blood being spilled. In the first decades after Christianity established itself in this region, it could not be stopped by any Roman persecution. In the absence of historical records, what took place in the years between 106 and 313, can only be the subject of speculation, but shortly after the recognition of Christianity, by Emperor Constantine, a great deal of church building activity began in the Negev. The construction of the Southern Church of Shivta might even have started as early as 330. The churches in the Negev are thus some of the oldest in the whole of Christianity and indicate that there were sufficient people in the region for whom the Christian sacrament was a regular religious requirement. The Nabateans were the first people who as a group declared their allegiance to Christianity. At the beginning, heathen cults continued to exist alongside Christianity, but later they increasingly merged with the Christian one.[19] Certainly, there are no indications of forced conversion to Christianity.[20]

The seventh century brought the Islamic invasion. The assumption of power by representatives of this new religious stream once again remained without military consequences for the region. Initially, good relations existed between the new rulers and church. In Shivta it can be clearly seen that care was taken not to damage a neighbouring church building during the construction of a mosque. Both places of worship co-existed peacefully over a long period of time. It was Islamic policy initially to support the church administration with the intention of separating it from the state — in accordance with the old Roman principle: Divide and rule. In the Negev, where the influence of those who held power had always been limited, this method only had one effect. A peaceful, hard-working population, economically well-off through the fruits of its own work, lived there, but later, as the hunger for power of the ruling Muslims continued to grow, the burden of taxes became increasingly heavy. The people increasingly lost their livelihood in a society which had in the meantime become completely agricultural. The burden of taxes no longer left room for any significant income and earnings from wine growing continued to decline due to the Islamic ban on alcohol.

A strongly Christian conviction did not provide a suitable base for a militant movement which could provide an effective defence. And although Nabatean history tells of many heroic battles — though almost without exception they were defensive ones — there was no significant resistance. The shine on their wealth began to tarnish; a well-organized society faced collapse.

In the northern part of the Holy Land, Christianity had in the meantime also won significant numbers of adherents. More than three hundred churches were built in the lands of Judea and Galilee within two hundred years. Many of those who were forced to leave their home, under the Roman persecution of Christians, found a new home in the Negev. During the heyday of Christian culture in the fourth and fifth centuries up to a hundred thousand people had lived in the Negev.[21] After the establishment of Muslim rule, increasing numbers of people emigrated, and the population declined. The cities were abandoned and began to crumble but were spared the fate of hostile destruction and plunder. No other civilization came to an end in such a peaceful way after being conquered.

The circle which lasted over thousand years now closed. In the long distant past it was nomads who brought a highly spiritual civilization to the Negev. Now it was once again nomadic shepherds who remained in the Negev and travelled through the desert with their herds in individual tribes. However, they no longer carried the seed of a new and forward-looking cultural development within them, and gradually they too acquired Islam and their descendants can be found among the Bedouin of the region to this day. Only a few ruins are left of the former glory of Nabatean culture — silent witnesses to an almost forgotten chapter of early Christianity.

CHAPTER THREE

Nabatean Religion and its Transformation

Tracing the origins and development of Nabatean religion is hampered by the lack of historical documentation, particularly for the early period.

The situation before the birth of Christ

The further we look back into the pre-Christian period, the more diverse the pantheon of Nabatean gods is, which presents itself. If Judaism was a religion which turned to a single God, the pre-Christian religion of the Nabateans belonged to paganism. Numerous spiritual beings who were involved in the creation of living things were still perceived in a pictorially imaginative fashion. The idea of the existence of a transcendental single Creator who could not be experienced directly was an alien concept to pagan religions. Only the development of the intellectual forces of consciousness enabled the transition to an abstract concept of God which could grasp the divine principle as a unity, and develop a monotheistic belief.[1] The Nabatean conception of the world was informed by numerous influences and impressions which — through their life as caravan traders — made its mark on their consciousness through constant contact with foreign cultures. Thus the attempt to present a specific *Nabatean* idea of God must fail due to the absence of a unified image of God; this took on various shades depending on time and place.

In academic studies today, the content of ancient religions is mostly observed from an inappropriately critical perspective. Everything which does not have a monotheistic base is described as *primitive*. This does not take into account that religious ideas and practices took different forms with the evolution of human consciousness. The people of classical antiquity not only lived differently from us, they *thought* and *felt* differently as well. Thus we must see a development in the transformation of the Nabatean image of God, in the course of which their understanding of the divine and their insight into extra-sensory existence was subject to constantly-evolving metamorphosis. Over the course of time, the perception of the divine was obscured into *knowledge,* of which in later times, only *belief* remained.[2] The vision stage cannot be described as a religion. *Re-ligio* means *re-connection.* Religious ceremonies were established to prevent the awareness of God's presence from dying away; to keep it alive under the guidance of priests.

Gnosticism and early Christianity

The way in which this *religio* was conducted by the Nabateans coupled with the emergence of Christianity, indicates a further unique feature of their civilization. It becomes apparent when we put it in the context of the distinction which Rudolf Steiner made between the pre-Christian mysteries and the Christian ritual:

> The Mystery of Golgotha, however, differs from all the other Mysteries ... [in that it stands] on the stage of history before the whole world, while the older Mysteries were enacted in the obscurity of the inner temples and sent out their impulses into the world from the dim twilight of these inner temples.[3]

Exactly the opposite appears to have been the case in Nabatean culture. The rituals and mysteries of the pre-Christian era took place outside in broad daylight, on mountain tops and other exposed places of the landscape. It was not until shortly before the birth of Christ that buildings were erected which moved the mystery cult inside. The first

Nabatean Christian churches from the fourth century in particular, appear to have reflected the characteristic features of pre-Christian mystery sites to a much greater extent. The basic Christian sacraments took place in the Negev and in the mountains of Petra, in closed buildings within which the half-light of the temple interior reigned. Thus the sacraments of early Christianity in the first centuries after the birth of Christ, were clearly seen as *mysteries.* Alexander Cruden writes: 'Mystery: the word signifies a secret; a mystery is something that is kept secret and remains hidden from our understanding until it is revealed to us.'[4]

Cruden distinguishes between mysteries which do not reveal themselves without prior initiation and others which are revealed, the content of which we know but which may still elude our immediate understanding. The latter applies to the Christian mysteries, to the phenomenon of the resurrection, the ascension of Christ or to St Paul's experience at the gates of Damascus.

Normally the mystery cult is considered to be a typical characteristic of pre-Christian religions, but as we can see from St Paul's writings, the sources of mystery wisdom had by no means dried up in the early Christian period.[5] In his letter to the Corinthians, he writes: 'This is how one should regard us, as servants of Christ, and stewards of the mysteries of God' (1Cor.4:1). The brilliance of the mysteries appeared to become muted with the birth of Christ, but the knowledge which was contained in the mysteries continued to exist. A new kind of spiritual revelation, *Gnosticism,* arose at the transition between the old religions and the rise of Christianity, which reflected the old mystery knowledge in a subtly transformed way.[6] It preserved elements of the knowledge in the consciousness of people at the time, which still echoed from the world of the old mysteries. In *The Gnostic Religion,* Hans Jonas writes that, in contrast to *belief,* Gnosticism meant:

> knowledge of God ... It comprises all those things which belong to the divine sphere of existence, namely the order and history of the higher worlds, and their consequences: the redemption of the human being.[7]

Gnosticism, which in exact translation means *knowledge,* was perceived as a threat by the institutionalized Church, which fought against it and persecuted it. Gnostic knowledge as it was widely distributed in the Orient at the time of the birth of Christ has therefore been preserved mainly in the polemics against it by the Church fathers.

Echoes of the mystery wisdom of Saba

Today, we believe that the Nabateans were originally a small tribal group which in the sixth century BC penetrated northwards from the kingdom of Saba, to the border regions of the agricultural lands, perhaps as the result of a natural catastrophe.[8] There are references to a Nabatean presence in the northern Arabian region in the eighth century BC both in the annals of Tiglath-pileser and in the Old Testament book of Job (1:15). From southern Arabian inscriptions, the only sources from which we have a picture of early Saba, we are familiar with the term *Mukharib,* meaning *the close one,* who as ruler of his people also exercised the office of High Priest.[9] His temporal position of leadership was based on his spiritual authority. This did not change until the Sabeo-Nabatean tribes left southern Arabia. A few centuries later, in the fifth century BC, the Mukharibs were replaced by kings, but the Nabatean rulers maintained their dual function in which there was still a clear balance in favour of their religious tasks.

We can speculate from some of these inscriptions that the principle of co-rulership also goes back to old Sabean traditions. Two blood relatives — father and son, or two brothers — stood at the head of the kingdom and ruled jointly. One was entrusted with all the political tasks in administering the kingdom, while the other was responsible for religious matters. Certain rituals of baptism as well as forms of monasticism, which did not only spread among the Nabateans in the post Christian era, had their origin in ritual forms which were older than Christianity; they played a key role in India in a Buddhist context as early as the sixth century BC. In the same period ritual baptism existed in Saba as well as a special form of monasticism.[10] Early Nabatean religion and spirituality must be seen as a direct continua-

Figure 6. Sabean altar, fifth to sixth century BC, depicting the sun disc cradled in the moon.

tion of the religious customs of Saba and its ritual practices. The Sabean world of the gods and its mysteries of the sun and the moon were taken by the Nabatean tribes during their emigration, into the desert south of the Holy Land.

In contrast to the Greeks, the Nabateans did not locate their gods in a place on earth. They lived in heaven, in the realm of the stars. Anyone turning to their gods raised their eyes to the heavens and sought their image there. It was a religion which revealed the three basic forces of existence — Sun, Moon and Stars — in their visible cosmic manifestation. The divine was reduced to a trinity, and in the early stages of the ninth and eighth centuries BC, spoke to human beings through natural phenomena. The sun as visible manifestation in the heavens was revered as a female God. The moon took on male characteristics, as did the morning or evening star which must be considered as the son — a complete contrast to the western tradition where it became Venus. The image of the bull was also linked to the moon. Both embodied aspects of fertility: the moon in its waxing and waning, the bull as a physical representation of power and vitality. To emphasize this aspect, the shape of bull horns often came close to the shape of the crescent moon, in which the sun rests and is carried like in a chalice (Figure 6). This ritual symbol may be a predecessor of the Grail motif as it was to appear at a later time in the Christian world.

Service in the temple was carried out by women and men, called *Lauwa.* The root of this word is the same as the Hebrew *Levi* (Levite), which means *companion* or *servant in the temple.* The gods were consulted in Sabean temples.[11] This cult of the oracle was continued by the Nabatean kings who were still filled with religious consciousness. Thus Stephen of Byzantium reports:

> Aretas began to question the oracle. The oracle said he should look for a place called Auara [anointed with gold?] ... And when Aretas arrived and lay awake, he saw a sign, a figure dressed in white riding on a white camel.[12]

The king referred to here is Aretas IV, the contemporary of Jesus of Nazareth. The words quoted above show clearly that questioning the oracle continued to be done by the Nabatean kings at the time of the birth of Christ, just as it had been done in the Sabean kingdom.

Religion under Hellenic influence

Saba, also called *Mysterion* by the Greeks, and later during the Roman period *Arabia Felix* — happy Arabia — consists largely of fertile mountain country. By contrast, the northern Arabian regions, the Negev and the Petran mountains, are bare and dry. The harsh living conditions in the desert meant constantly having to deal with the issue of survival. People who have lived there for generations have developed an intimate connection with and a subtle sense of everything which makes existence in the desert possible and which enables

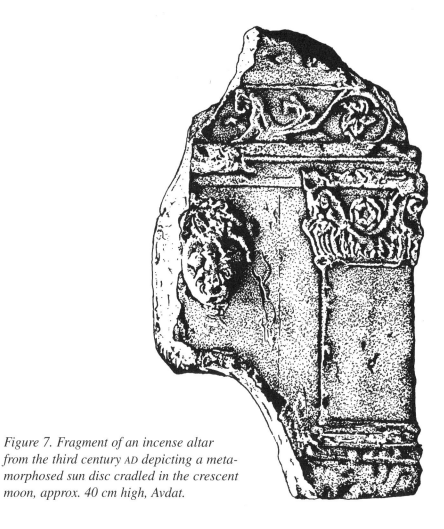

Figure 7. Fragment of an incense altar from the third century AD *depicting a metamorphosed sun disc cradled in the crescent moon, approx. 40 cm high, Avdat.*

life to grow, sprout and flourish. This also produced an enhanced perception of the way in which the divine works in nature.

Following Sabean tradition, the sun mysteries which were celebrated in the early Nabatean period from the sixth to the first half of the fourth century BC, took place in the open air. Static buildings were still not being constructed. Ritual acts were carried out on the road in provisional encampments. Just as each sensory impression was perceived more strongly in the monotony of the desert, the influence of the natural phenomena which corresponded to the gods — sun, moon and stars — had a particularly intense and direct effect on human beings in this environment. However, the influence of cosmic forces was not only experienced in the external phenomenon of growth, in the way that the life forces developed, but also in their spiritual effect. They were so intense for Nabatean consciousness that divine beings were able to maintain their existence outside the human sphere.

Following the campaign of Alexander the Great the whole of the East, including Nabatean shepherds and caravan traders, was increasingly exposed to Hellenic influences. From a religious perspective, the time until then could be called an *archaic* age, but a new phase now began which can be described as the *classical* one.

The further we look back into the past, the fewer sources of information there are, and the less clear the picture becomes. Nevertheless, descriptions in more recent documents can sometimes give glimpses through which we can gain an insight into earlier periods. Thus Strabo reports: 'They [the Nabateans] worship the sun and build altars on the roofs of their houses where they place drink and make smoke sacrifices.'[13] While this description is of a situation shortly before the birth of Christ, when the Nabateans started building houses, it also throws light on very ancient cultic traditions, and show how deeply rooted the sun cult was.

Archeological finds from this period also allow us to draw certain conclusions. Continuity in the depiction of the gods (see Figures 6, 7 and 13) can be observed right down to the shape of the altars. The head of the bull as symbol of the moon, the moon chalice and the sun it carries, are eternal images which reflect the transition of religious experience from the archaic to the classical era.

Now the Nabatean image of the gods began to change. The gods moved closer to human beings. Their home, which was located in the far distant heavens in archaic times, was increasingly characterized by earthly features. *Sharay* is 'a place with dense vegetation were wild animals graze,' a kind of paradise. *Dushara,* the name of the main Nabatean god, means 'Master of Sharay.'[14] Stephen of Byzantium explains that *Aara* is the name of a rock which was named after this God. *Shara* is also the name for the Edom mountains. Dushrat or

Figure 8. The high place of sacrifice on a mountain south of Petra.

Dushara (*Dusares* in Greek) was no longer expressly a sun god. Metaphorically speaking, he descended to the summit of the mountains. Initially he is linked with the mountains as such, similarly to Yahweh who revealed himself on Mount Sinai. Later, however, he appears to take up residence on a specific mountain near Petra, the Jebel esh-Sharat. Several inscriptions also describe him as 'God of Gaia' or 'God of Medrasa.' In a Hellenistically moulded and transformed consciousness, it was now possible to experience Dushara as a personal and individual God. In Arabic, *Aara* means 'the anointed one without compare.' *Dushrat* or *Dushara* is therefore also the 'anointed one' — which means nothing other than the Hebrew word *Messiah,* or the Greek, *Christos.*

Maximus of Tyre comments in the second century AD: 'The Arabs serve I know not whom, but I saw his statue which was a square stone.'[15] This is one of the oldest eyewitness accounts which indicates that the god Dushrat did not take an anthropomorphic form although he had come closer to the Hellenistic ideal. The *Suda Lexicon,* which was compiled at the end of the tenth century, also refers to older sources which have since been lost, and provides a similar picture:

> Theus Ares [Dushrat]; this is the god Ares in Arabic Petra. They worship the god Ares and venerate him above all. His statue is an unworked square black stone. It is four foot high and two wide. It rests on a golden base. They make sacrifices to him and before him they anoint the blood of the sacrifice; that is their anointment ...[16]

As well as a large number of idols and divine images, there is a place of sacrifice (Figure 8) on a mountain south of the valley of Petra where there are indications that mysteries and sacrificial rituals were celebrated in the open air. The spiritual beings who were venerated here are manifested in the celestial bodies; sun, moon and stars. The walls of rock on the steep, narrow path which finishes 1050 metres above sea level, is lined by numerous idols which have been carved into the rock. The changing appearance of these depictions of the gods makes this climb appear like a journey through the various ages of Nabatean history and allows us to see the development of their idea of the divine up to the Christian period. Whereas only a limited amount of sky is visible at the bottom of the valley in which the city of antiquity lies hidden, we see the whole of the heavenly vault from the summit. There are no further depictions of the gods at the place of sacrifice itself, one of the oldest in the Nabatean region. If the gods were already perceived in the surrounding elements during the stren-uous climb, they were revealed all the more intensely during the open air ritual ceremony.

The later the time when the idols and monuments were made, the more often they possess an interior space. The place of sacrifice, sit-uated at a high level, is completely open — there is an unhindered view to the horizon in all directions. The rock monuments which were built in the second and first centuries BC, now begin to conquer the vertical plane. The wall idols form an intermediate step, sculpted in

Figure 9. Niche monument with the stele of a Nabatean deity (Dushrat) in the early non-figurative style.

Figure 10. Avdat, Nabatean acropolis with the ruins from the Byzantine period.

stone, sometimes only forty to fifty centimetres high, giving only a hint of the three dimensional without actually taking hold of space (see Figure 9).

Whereas the Greek gods took human forms, appeared among people and sometimes even married them, there was no such relationship to the world of the gods among the Nabateans. Such an artistic depiction of divine beings and divine qualities would have been completely alien to their mythological consciousness. The same tendency can be found in Judaism in a more extreme way. There we find an

Figure 11. Stele (betyl) of a deity with stylized human face, probably first century BC, Petra.

absolute ban on images of God. One of the ten commandments is: 'You shall not make for yourself a graven image, or any likeness ...' (Exod. 20:4). Despite these parallels, completely different reasons lay behind the rejection by the Nabateans of pictorial depictions of the gods. In Judaism, the lack of a physical presence of God was compensated by the development of an intellectual potential which made it possible to have a *concept,* if not an *image,* of God. For the Nabateans, on the other hand, an image of a divine being must have appeared superfluous since its presence was perceived on quite a different plane from the physical.

For Nabatean consciousness before the birth of Christ, the gods had descended from the heavens to the summits of the mountains, but were still far from human perception. Only in the final phase of the classical period did they receive faces, which were, however, still only hinted at and strongly stylized (Figure 11). Previously, there had only been stone markers which did not symbolize the gods themselves but only the place of their presence. Such idols were described in contemporary Greek writings as *betyl.* This term has its origins in the Semitic root *beth-el* which can be described as the *house of God.* Some of these divine images come from a time when the Nabateans did not yet possess homes made of stone. The first to live in stone dwellings among the Nabateans were thus the gods. First the gods were given accommodation, only then did they build solid dwellings for themselves.

Betyls can be various sizes. The older ones are in a niche in which a block-like relief can be seen. Others contain two or three reliefs of various sizes;[17] the one on the right is usually a little smaller (Figure 9). In more recent periods, eyes, nose and mouth can be clearly distinguished, but even with these few features the limit of figurative depiction is reached with a few exceptions (Figure 12) — this did not change in later periods either.[18] Where the gods do appear in their full form, such as the finds at Khirbet et-Tannur, the Hellenistic influence appears to have become so powerful that there must be some doubt as to whether we are dealing with members of the same religion, or a dying branch of the Nabatean religion which did not lead to Christianity.[19]

Figure 12. Medallion betyl of Dushrat on the path to the place of sacrifice, Petra. In contrast to the plinth, the deity already appears in human form on the upper part of the stele, which was presumably created at a later time.

Identifying Nabatean depictions of the gods

In the absence of inscriptions giving any indication of names, Nelson Glueck — who contributed much to research about the Nabateans and their environment — attempted to use other attributes to identify the gods depicted in various statues and reliefs, which he found at sites

Figure 13. Rock stele of the Goddess Allat near Ein esh-Shellaleh. Although a first step towards anthropomorphic representation is recognizable, the Nabatean motifs of the chalice and the sun disc also recur.

east of Wadi Araba.[20] In doing so, he draws mainly on parallels with the depiction of deities by neighbouring peoples. Khirbet et-Tannur where most of these statues of deities were found, is situated on the border of Nabatea, far from the major trade routes, close to a base of Greek colonial forces. It is quite feasible that a cult of local deities developed there which assimilated the influences of neighbouring civilizations, and became separated from the mainstream of Nabatean religion. Avraham Negev points out that there is no written documentation to back up the names given to the deities by Glueck.[21]

One exception, in which a deity can clearly be identified as *Zeus Obodas* from accompanying inscriptions, originates in the third century AD and was discovered in Avdat (Oboda).[22] Such a classification is also confirmed by a mention in Stephen of Byzantium's *Ethnica:* 'Oboda ..., where King Obodas, whom they venerated as a god, is buried.'[23] Oboda (now Avdat), a city with a large Nabatean acropolis (Figures 10 and 12) received its name from King Obodas III who was elevated to the rank of a deity in accordance with Roman custom. *Zeus Obodas* is mentioned in all inscriptions in connection with commemoration of the dead.

The Nabatean pantheon and its gods

In the last centuries before the birth of Christ, vineyards were established in the Negev under the rule of the last Nabatean king, Rabel II. Less than three hundred years earlier, the planting of vines and the drinking of wine had been a crime punishable by death. Apart from the significance of wine in religious ceremonies, vines are characterized by their great capacity to survive and their vitality. These life forces were supposed to be transferred to the participants in the religious act.

As the life-giving god, Dushrat now also became the god of the vine. The features which characterize the vine among plants corresponded to the effect of Dushrat in a human context. In the fifth century, the Byzantine writer Hesychios described him as 'Dionysos of the Nabateans.' However, as the god of wine he never appears to have achieved the same kind of reputation as his Greek counterpart. Ecstatic or orgiastic elements never gained a foothold in the religious ceremonies of the Nabateans. The Greek god Dionysos, called Bacchus by the Romans, was considered in Greek mythology to be the son of Zeus. Dushrat, in contrast, as the sun god and representative of a spiritual current which had its origins in the succession of the Sabean sun mysteries, was venerated as the son of a virgin.[24] His birth was celebrated on 6 January, the same day as the Epiphany in the Christian calendar. The Christmas festival of the Armenian Church, of which Nabatean Christianity was later to become a part, is still celebrated on this day.

Memorials to Dushrat have also been found in Avdat. Here in the Negev, as well as in central Arabia, he was venerated as the god of growth and plants, and stone steles were erected to him which were set up in niches. Several such steles can be found near Avdat on the walls of the underground cisterns dating from Nabatean times of which there are a fair number in the Negev. There Dushrat became the patron of water which, in the words of Avraham Negev, 'is as important in the desert as the blood of human beings.'[25]

In contrast to Nelson Glueck, Avraham Negev thinks that there were significantly few Nabatean deities.[26] Many of the other gods which were venerated in the region of Nabatea — such as *al-Kutba,* goddess of writing; *Qaus,* the Edomite god of the weather, storms and lightning; *Manat,* goddess of fate, related to the Greek Tyche — are all outsiders in the Nabatean pantheon. They were admitted as part of syncretizing developments (unifying the different schools of thought) and Nabatean openness towards the world. *Shaj al-Qaum* must, on the other hand, have been an important deity, if we go by the number of inscriptions and memorials which have been found in the whole of the Nabatean region. His name means *leader of the armies.* We know from the Old Testament that this can also refer to the heavenly hosts which had their physical manifestation in the stars. The stars in the sky were understood by the peoples of antiquity as signs of divine will which could be interpreted from the constellations.

Whereas Dushrat was considered to be a god of daytime, linked with the sun, Shaj al-Qaum was seen as a night-time god protecting the souls of sleepers, accompanying them in their nightly journey through the heavenly realms, and guiding caravans in the desert by means of the stars. An inscription in Palmyra in Syria describes him as the god 'who drinks no wine,' thus acting as a counterbalance to the Dionysian features of Dushrat.[27]

The large number of inscriptions bearing the name of the goddess

Figure 14. Triclinium opposite the Soldier's Tomb, Petra.

Allat support the idea that she was the most important female deity of the Nabateans. The majority of these inscriptions were found at the periphery of the kingdom. One exception is the site by a spring with the name Ein esh-Shellaleh, near Petra. A niche with a *betyl* representing the goddess has written above it the words: 'This is the goddess Allat of Bostra.' The depiction on the memorial shows a schematic drawing of a human form which appears to rise on a crescent moon (Figure 13). Bostra was situated in the extreme north of the kingdom (now called Bosra). Allat was venerated as a goddess mainly in the northern Arabian region and is therefore not of Nabatean origin. Only in a later period of Roman predominance does she receive

Figure 15. Obelisk Tomb, first century AD, *Petra. The entrance to the triclinium is in the lower storey.*

her place among the Nabatean deities. Herodotus calls her 'the goddess of all Arabs' and equates her with the Greco-Roman goddess Aphrodite or Venus.

The most ancient reference to the goddess *al-Uzza,* 'the powerful one,' originates in the fourth century BC, the first time that the Nabateans are mentioned in classical history. An inscription in Nabatean and Greek which contains her name and equated her with Aphrodite was found on the Aegean island of Kos.[28] Nevertheless, al-Uzza appears to have been originally a Nabatean deity who only gradually took on the features of a Greek goddess. Avraham Negev notes in this respect that the power which comes to expression in the name of the goddess is linked to the morning star, and that a relationship can be established between her and Venus (Aphrodite) on the astral level.[29] St Jerome in the fourth century, describes a festival of al-Uzza, the morning star, which was celebrated in Elusa. Al-Uzza rituals, which were practised in Mecca and which only disappeared once Islam had established itself, are also mentioned in early Islamic documents. According to his own evidence, Muhammad himself was a follower of the goddess in his youth and made sacrifices to her. Such few inscriptions as there are, and *betyls* which are almost identical, allow us to assume that in the border regions of the kingdom al-Uzza and Allat were considered to be a single deity with two names.

Dushrat, the sun god, Sahj el-Qaum, the male god of the night, and al-Uzza, the goddess of the stars, were the most important members of the Nabatean pantheon. They appear as representatives of the divine world as it existed in the imagination of Nabatean emigrants from Saba. The transformation and development of Nabatean consciousness after the departure from Saba — brought about not least through contact with Judaic messianic expectations and the influence of Greek culture — meant that they were transformed into *Hellenomorphic* deities with human characteristics.

According to the way of thinking at the time, divine characteristics took on pictorial forms which resulted in similarities with the Olympian gods. In contrast to the Greeks, however, the mythological consciousness of the Nabateans maintained a certain distance from the spiritual beings which they venerated. Nabateans still looked upwards when they turned to the divine world whereas the Greeks encountered the gods at eye level.

The Nabateans were particularly sensitive in relation to the life forces at work in human beings and nature, which is described by Rudolf Steiner as the *etheric* world.[30] The perception of these finer processes and their action in the divine world was experienced differently from the Greeks, where the depiction of the gods could no longer be distinguished from those of human beings. The Nabateans encountered their gods within themselves, in the soul — and that is where they spoke to them. They did not first have to assume human form in order to be perceived. On the contrary, they revealed themselves in the balance between a purely spiritual and a physical existence. The Nabateans before the birth of Christ encountered their gods at the threshold where the divine will in the spirit seeks to take on physical form, where a spiritual intention becomes a formative force before it comes to expression in the act of creation.

Nabatean religious buildings

The earliest Nabatean buildings were temples. Before they could be built, leave had to be taken from a long-held tradition in which there was no place for the construction of fixed buildings made of stone, and where such activity was subject to punishment. It is still not certain why the sudden turn to architecture occurred. Even more puzzling is the fact that Nabatean architecture, both religious and secular, displays a high level of technical and artistic skill right from the beginning. In a nomadic culture one would normally expect a development from simple tent constructions to temple architecture to take place in many small stages.

A few decades before the birth of Christ, the construction of religious stone sites was started everywhere in the Negev. Their remains can be found in Petra, Avdat and Khirbet et-Tannur; others are thought to exist in Elusa, Nessana and Ruheiba under the ruins of Christian churches. The previous rites which once took place under the open sky were now transferred to the inside of buildings.

The *Qasr al-Bint Farun* — a name which was invented by Bedouin at a later time — is considered to be the most important temple in Petra and must in earlier times have dominated the cityscape as the largest structure (Figure 16). This building, which was created at the time of Christ, is described in the tenth century *Suda Lexicon* as Temple of *Theus Ares* (Dushrat). Originally fronted with marble and stucco, it must have been a work of monumental beauty. Its position in the shadow of the huge *Umm al-Biyara* rock (mother of springs) puts it in an opposite position to the place of sacrifice on the mountain. The rites which took place here show evidence of a new and more intimate relationship between human beings and deity. Both

Figure 16. Qasr al-Bint Farun, built at the time of Christ. The former city temple of Petra was dedicated to the main Nabatean god, Dushrat.

now have their encounter in an interior space where a *religio,* a reconnection of the human soul with its divine origin, could take place.

This transition of the religious space to the inside introduced the third era of their religion to the Nabateans — the Christian one. The Mystery of Golgotha comes closer. The expectation of redemption by the spiritual world grew stronger in many of the classical civilizations. The presence of the divine was found less and less in the external world, the dialogue with the deity took place only in the interior of the human soul. Human beings were increasingly challenged to develop such a relationship for themselves. The withdrawal of the divine from the world placed an increasing responsibility for the progress of human development on to human beings, but there was also an awareness of the inability to do justice to this task by human strength alone. The unity with the spiritual world was destroyed. Its restoration can be considered as the actual meaning of the Mystery of Golgotha.

The merging of architectural styles

The area where the Nabateans lived was the meeting point between East and West. As caravan drivers, its inhabitants moved between India and Europe, Yemen and Egypt, Arabia and the Mediterranean. They came into contact with all kinds of different peoples and lifestyles, and had the remarkable ability to assimilate elements from other cultures, without forcible exploitation or military conquest.

The few reports which do exist and which shed some light on religious customs at the royal court, indicate a special ceremony with its own unique Nabatean character. Architectural style, ornaments and crafts, by contrast, contained elements of foreign cultures from as far away as India. In historical research, this phenomenon — the integration of stylistic characteristics from various origins, particularly in the world under the influence of Greek civilization — is described as *syncretism.* It is often thought to accompany a certain cultural decadence. The unstoppable spread of Hellenistic culture was only possible, according to this view, because it encountered less developed peoples. The world of the Greek gods is thought to have replaced local deities. Gods which had become weak were removed from office.

Syncretism can, however, also be interpreted from a different point of view. In the world of antiquity there was an expectation of redemption through the *anointed one,* the *Christos, Messiah* or *Aara.* A strange *spirit presence* was perceived by the peoples of various civilizations. This is evident in the fact that at the same time gnostic currents emerged everywhere through which eastern wisdom flowed into the thinking of Mediterranean peoples.[31] Gnosis means *knowledge,* and it was intended to be the means to achieve *religio,* the re-establishment of the connection between spiritual elements in human beings and the divine world. Hellenism was the cultural medium through which true spirituality was able to produce fruits in other, unrelated cultures as well. The syncretism of the time must therefore be understood as an awakening in the spirituality of neighbouring cultures, and not merely as the external acquisition of foreign cultural elements.

This ability to transform something alien into something of one's own was particularly strongly developed among the Nabateans. The ethnic diversity of the population also played a role. As we have seen during the last centuries before the birth of Christ, the population of the Negev consisted of a colourful mixture of various civilizations of the classical world,[32] who were at this time, probably in control of the greatest material riches in the whole of the Mediterranean area. Cultural multiplicity and extreme wealth are likely to have the formed basis for the development of a spirituality from which a new, contemporary religious consciousness was able to emerge.

Tomb monuments and the cult of the dead

Petra, the capital of the Nabateans, was the cultural and religious centre of the whole kingdom. Many domestic buildings have been excavated, but the striking feature is the number of monuments which exist in relation to secular buildings. The religious architecture, which arose earlier than purely utilitarian buildings, shows typical characteristics. It consisted of:

Monuments which were hewn out of the rock face, whose religious significance is not in doubt

Traditional temple buildings

Triclinia, often also described as *tomb Triclinia*[33]

Theatres which were erected in direct proximity to a necropolis

In the view of Avraham Negev temple rites consisted of two key elements: the procession to the Temple, on whose roof the sacrifice — animal and incense — was made, as well as the ritual banquet which was held in the nearby theatre.[34]

In Petra, as well as in other Nabatean settlements, there are many *triclinia* which were used for religious purposes.[35] A *triclinium* consists of a rectangular room with benches on three walls (*triclinium* means 'three benches'). In ancient Greece, they were used to celebrate sacrificial banquets, followed by a symposium — as we know from Plato's writings of the same name from the fourth century BC. A symposium in the Greek style is a philosophical discussion dealing with questions and problems of *religio*. Only with the Romans did the philosophical discussions decline during the gathering in the triclinium, which then often served purely social purposes. The architectural idea of the triclinium was taken over by the Nabateans because it accorded with their particular type of syncretism. Many of the triclinia in Petra did not, however, consisted of stonework, but were hewn into the rock (Figure 14). In Greek triclinia, each room had three rows of pillars which were essential to support the ceiling. The pillars were arranged such that they did not block the view of the landscape on the open side. In Petran cave-like triclinia, such a construction was not necessary. The pillars were included for purely decorative purposes and were moved behind the rows of seats where they decorated the walls as reliefs in the form of half-pillars or pilasters. The floor of the interior has rectangular depressions, which are also found in the rooms of the hollowed-out rock monuments. Cultic pottery was found in the triclinia which are similar to ceramics found in the cemeteries of other sites, such as Elusa. This shows with certainty that the Petran triclinia were connected with the cult of the dead.

The so-called *tomb monuments* of Petra were created between the first century BC and the end of the second century AD. Neither skeletons nor other additions to the tombs have ever been found in them. Academics believe that they were robbed in later times. However, the assumption that these are tombs in the conventional sense in which the body of the deceased was buried is contradicted by a report by Strabo: 'They [the Nabateans] consider dead bodies no better than dung, as Heraklitos says: ... corpses are more despicable than dung. And therefore they bury even their kings beside dung heaps.'[36]

If Strabo's report contains the truth, the construction of such mighty monuments cannot be reconciled with his description of the lack of respect in handling the physical remains of the dead. There are also differences of opinion about the date when this monumental style originated. The first systematic descriptions of these monuments date from 1897 and 1898, by two German scientists, Brünnow and Domaszewski, during their stay in Petra. They dated its origins to the fourth century BC.[37] More recent research does not consider the various types of monuments to represent a chronological sequence but explains their peculiarities as the result of the likes and dislikes of their respective builders.

The term *tomb monument* must be used with the greatest care in the context of this type of architecture. For a desert culture of former nomads, who avoided being tied to any particular place in any way, the places where their dead were buried could not have had any great religious significance. If they had, it would have been necessary visit them at regular intervals in order to celebrate the cult of the dead, to look after sites and if necessary defend them. There will most certainly have been deaths on the long journeys through the desert, but the hot climate did not permit the deceased to be transported for any length of time due to their rapid decomposition. They had to be buried locally. That is why Strabo's report appears to be a true reflection of reality. Where people do not remember their dead in specific places, it is no surprise that a cult of the dead should be much more spiritual in outlook, and that locality should play only a secondary role. Life after death was self-evident for the people of antiquity, as examples from all ancient civilizations show. Fawzi Zayadine distinguishes eight different types of tomb in Petra.[38] Some of them were undoubtedly tombs in the conventional sense, but these originated at a later time when the population of Petra had grown in number and with it the requirement for burial sites.

One of these types of tomb is the *stele monument* (Figure 15). This is an obelisk-type structure above a triclinium which is similar to the free-standing obelisks which we will refer to below. In the language of the Nabateans they are called *nephsha* [*N-Ph-Sh*], as inscriptions show. Zayadine remarks on the importance of this name: *Nephesh* [*N-Ph-Sh*] has many different meanings in the Semitic languages. In biblical Hebrew the word means soul, life, person. It might also be translated as 'life principle' or 'feeling life ...'[39]

That *nephesh* monuments are not tombs in which corpses were buried is also confirmed by Zayadine. They were memorials where, by religious and mystical means, people combined the *nephesh* of the deceased with life forces. In most cases this took place in front of the *nephesh* monument and moved to the interior of the triclinia only at a later period. The enclosed space which occurs in the magnificent monument of *Al-Khasneh Farun* (commonly known in English as the *Treasury)* marks the latest stage of this development (Figures 44 and 46). There, too, ceremonies took place through which those who were present were to be enabled to have a mystical vision of the soul of the deceased. The physical body was of no importance for this rite. Some of these *mystery sites* recall Egyptian stylistic forms in the upper part of their façade owing to their relief-like battlements and steps, which describe a gesture of ascent and descent of the soul of the deceased (Figure 51). Despite these individual Egyptian echoes, there was no Nabatean rite of mummification. The idea of resurrection took a different form in their religious consciousness from the Egyptians. Their connection with the *life principle* prevented the Nabateans from worshipping physical objects — a further example of the Nabatean style of selective syncretism.

One riddle which remains unsolved for archeologists are the freestanding obelisks which are frequently found in Petra. They point to the heavens but no meaningful explanation of their significance has yet been found because of a lack of any inscriptions. Such free-standing obelisks from the same period have also been preserved in India. There they were called *stambha* and were an image for the supersensory presence of a deity.[40] Similar rock tombs are found also in India which were created as early as the lifetime of Buddha (sixth century BC). Nabatean caravans often penetrated as far as India and we may therefore assume a direct influence from this culture.[41]

The *Theatre* in Petra was carved into the rock on the southern slope of the valley. Several graves were destroyed during its construction — further evidence of the lack of concern about the physical remains of those who were buried there. The Nabatean theatre, although built in accordance with Greco-Roman models, also served ritual purposes. Both in Petra and in Elusa, the only Nabatean theatre west of Wadi Avdat, large numbers of broken pieces of typical Nabatean eggshell pottery associated with death cults, were found during excavations. They provide further evidence of the ritual banquets which were celebrated in the theatre, which was situated close to the temples and necropolises, not only in Petra but everywhere where Nabateans lived. There is, for once, agreement among researchers that the theatres were used for the ritual connected with existence after death.

The banquets for the those ritual assemblies in which about five thousand people could take part in the theatre in Petra, took place in the early morning to welcome the rising sun. The sun played an important role in the Nabatean Dushrat religion. The theatre in Petra faces north-east following the topography of the valley. When the people gathered in the morning for a ritual event, they looked in this direction. The facing rock wall hid the rising sun until relatively late in the day, even in the summer months, thus preventing the assembled crowds from being blinded by direct sunlight. The theatre in Elusa is situated in close proximity to a Nabatean temple which is assumed to be beneath the atrium of the Western Church.[42] It lies on the north-west axis. Here too the religious community could gather early in the morning and partake of the religious banquet without being blinded by the rising sun. The course and the content of this religious ceremony is no longer known, but the partaking of food as an image for spiritual events is not only recorded in Nabatean cultural history, but also in Christianity, where it became the centrepiece of religious ceremonies.

At the time of Christ, the religious centre of the Essenes was in Qumran, an oasis adjacent to the Dead Sea. The Essenes had separated themselves from conventional Judaism, and had built up a community in the wilderness based on strict religious principles. They also lived among the ordinary population, but like Petra, which was about sixty miles away, this settlement provided the focus of their religious life. An extraordinary amount of scientific attention has been paid to the spiritual legacy left by this community, particularly after the discovery of the scrolls written by them. Whether or not Christianity is rooted in the Essene world view, whether or not Jesus of Nazareth was influenced by their community, are questions which we will not investigate further here. However, the scrolls, which contain the communal regulations of the order, show that religious banquets, comparable to one of the basic Christian sacraments, were celebrated against the background of a heightened expectation of the arrival of the Messiah.

> The community council contains twelve people and three priests, pure in all respects and familiar with everything which the Torah can reveal. They follow truth and are charitable and just, they love mercy and are modest in each other's company. And when they gather together at table, and the table of the community is laid for the consumption of wine and bread, no one will reach for the bread basket and the wine before the priest has done so, for he will first bless the bread and then the Messiah of Israel will reach for the bread and then the community of Israel will bless the bread, each one according to his honour.[43]

The Essenes withdrew from civilization in order to live their lives in absolute purity in expectation of the Redeemer, because civilization appeared decadent to them. Similar customs were observed by Strabo, an objective contemporary by all appearances, at the Nabatean royal court:

> Since they [the Nabateans] keep few slaves, they are mostly served by relatives or serve one another. This habit even includes their kings. They prepare common meals for thirteen persons each and there are two musicians at each meal ... The king even condescends to serves the others as well as himself ...[44]

There can be no doubt that these customs were of religious significance in the sense of the equality of all citizens before the divine world. The habits at the communal meal also gave it a religious meaning. They were intended to transmit the idea that the life-giving force in nature was divine in origin.

There are no clear historical reports about direct religious contacts between Judea and Nabatea. Whereas the Nabateans were keen to assimilate spiritual truths which they encountered in other cultures, Judean documents make almost no reference to foreign cultural possessions. The analytical attitude of Judaism meant that almost all traces of existing spiritual links to non-Jewish cultures were removed. One of the few exceptions can be found in the *Jerusalem Talmud.*[45] This mentions a woman by the name of Kimchit who is praised for her two fine sons — both High Priests of Jerusalem. It is mentioned in passing (which is probably why it escaped the censor) that Simon, one of these sons who held the office of High Priest at the time, took a walk in Jerusalem with an Arab king on the eve of Yom Kippur, the holiest day of the Jewish calendar. Judea was at that time surrounded by the Nabatean kingdom. From a Judean perspective *Arab* was equivalent to *Nabatean,* as we have already seen. Simon, Kimchit's son, must have held office for one year at some time between AD 15 and 26. He was thus a contemporary of Jesus.[46] The Arab king mentioned here can be none other than Aretas IV, who was given the epithet *Philodemos,* 'he who loves his people,' who ruled from 9 BC to AD 40, and who, according to Stephen of Byzantium's report, saw a rider dressed in white riding on a camel in a vision (see p.65).

Yom Kippur is the only day of the year when the high priest is allowed to enter the Holy of Holies in the Temple. Why should an Nabatean king from Petra be in Jerusalem on such an evening? Why did he not meet the temporal rulers of the country instead of the High Priest, who had numerous religious ceremonies to fulfil on the eve of the holiest of Jewish days, and would have been occupied with baptisms, cleansing ceremonies, prayers, the selection of the sacrificial animals and the preparation of the sacrifice? What was the content of their conversation? All of these things remain riddles. We can only assume that there were firm relations between these two office holders and that religious topics were discussed. If the Nabatean king had not already heard about Jesus of Nazareth from the Essenes, we can assume with a considerable degree of certainty that he knew of him through his direct contact to the Temple in Jerusalem, for Jesus may not have been unknown in the ranks of the priests.

The dawn of the Christian era

The largest part of the material legacy of the Nabateans, left to a posterity eager to learn about them, comes from the Christian era. Much which could provide information about their religion and state of soul during the previous centuries remains hidden under the ruins of later buildings. A gradual but steady process of Christianization took place in various settlements, particularly those in the Negev, following the Mystery of Golgotha. Nabatean shrines were turned into churches, the gathering place in front of the temple now became an atrium. Unprecedented building activity began. Secular architecture for housing, which only began at a relatively late stage, began to take an important place, too. Domestic buildings were constructed in large numbers in all settlements. This shows clearly that the Nabateans had abandoned their nomadic existence.

The fact that they became increasingly settled is one of the three most important processes which occurred almost simultaneously in the history of the Nabateans in the decades around the time of Christ. In addition, the foundations were laid for the extraordinary development of agriculture in the third and fourth centuries; a start was made in reclaiming the desert. If in this context we talk about the maturity of the earth, it must be understood both in a literal and a metaphorical sense. Using spades, the earth was changed; its powers of growth were put to use and its fertility nurtured. Previously, the surface of the earth had only provided the ground on which people walked, and little attempt was made to change or develop it. From now on, the earth with its fruits made an important contribution to the existence of the Nabateans. However, in doing so, it also tied people to itself and guided them towards a maturity which required not only stamina and planning with regard to the harvest, but also an organized communal life which had special requirements under desert conditions. This spiritual and social maturity created the conditions for the third great renewal: the profession of faith in the newly emerging world religion — Christianity.

Pauline Christianity

Saul, who was to become the apostle Paul, was a prominent Pharisee who was initiated into Jewish law and the mystically-based knowledge of his religious community. He was a radical opponent of the view that the prophecy of the coming of the Messiah had been fulfilled in Jesus of Nazareth. On the way to Damascus, however, he had a crucial experience which transformed him from an opponent of Christianity into one of its most important proclaimers:

> Now as he journeyed, he approached Damascus, and suddenly there a light from heaven flashed about him: And he fell to the ground, and heard a voice saying to him, 'Saul, Saul, why do you persecute me?' And he said, 'Who are you Lord?' And He said, 'I am Jesus whom you are persecuting.' (Acts 9:3-5)

This experience was to be the starting point for Pauline Christianity,[47] which was based not only on the teaching but also on the inner experience of the resurrected Christ: 'It is sown a physical body, it is raised a spiritual body. If there is a physical body, there is also a spiritual body' (1Cor.15:44)

At the time that Paul arrived there, Damascus was under Nabatean rule. Thus the Second Epistle to the Corinthians says: 'At Damascus the governor under King Aretas guarded the city of Damascus in order to seize me.' (2Cor.11:32) This measure was directed at Saul's anti-Christian activities, as he intended to preach against the Christians in the synagogue in Damascus, on the instructions of the Jewish High Priest.

After the events at the gates of Damascus, Paul, in his own words, did not immediately return to Jerusalem, where in his new belief he might have expected to meet people of a similar mind to himself:

> ... that I might preach him among the Gentiles, I did not confer with flesh and blood, nor did I go up to Jerusalem to those who

were apostles before me; but I went away into Arabia; and
again I returned to Damascus. (Gal.1:16f)

From a Judean perspective there was only one Arabia at that time,
namely the one of the Nabateans. If we take Paul's words seriously,
he lived for three years among the Nabateans, and is likely to have
been received very positively with his new message. A transformation
such as Paul underwent would not have been unusual for the
Nabateans. At a cultural level they had undergone several transformations and were undergoing them again with the transition to
Christianity. For the Nabateans, the events at Damascus described by
Paul must have appeared like the fulfilment of what they had been
foretold by the mysteries. Only once *Aara* had been born, a happening which occurred not only externally but as an inward experience
and spiritual revelation, were all the conditions fulfilled for the start
of a new phase of Nabatean cultural development. From that time onwards, the divine world was present internally, in the human soul.

In such an environment, Paul was able to consolidate his new view
of the world and God before embarking on his missionary journeys to
the Mediterranean area. Since there are insufficient records regarding
Nabatean religious thought, we are, unfortunately, not in a position to
judge which specific elements of Nabatean spirituality influenced
Paul and the extent to which Pauline Christianity was marked by
Nabatean culture.

The Kings from the Orient

The lack of historical documentation has also meant that another
question of relevance of Christianity cannot be answered with total
certainty: who were the wise men from the Orient who stood at the
manger in Bethlehem?

In medieval traditions of esoteric Christianity, particularly among
the Rosicrucians, it was told that the Three Kings who followed the
Star and knew about the birth of Christ came from *Arabia Felix,* the
former Saba.[48] Nabatean civilization was largely based on elements of
the religion and mysteries which had been brought from their former

southern Arabian home, and which continued to be cultivated until the transition to Christianity. Only with the spread of Islam were these traditions allowed to fall into oblivion, and a break occur in the continuity of cultural development. In his reflections, S. von Gleich writes:

> In this way Islam cast obscurity on the history of a bright heathen and Arab civilization which started at least two thousand years before Muhammad ..., which made the transition into Sabean civilization in the age of Solomon and which prepared Christianity in a spiritual flowering without compare — just as, conversely, Islamic Arabism after Christ seriously endangered the early development of Christianity and unfavourably influenced its later Occidental development.[49]

Nabatean religion expected and longed for the spiritual impulses brought by Christianity and it is likely that a knowledge of the coming of the birth of Christ existed in the mysteries. This also casts some light on the words of the Gospel of St Matthew (2:2): 'For we have seen his star in the East, and have come to worship him.' In the absence of any records, we can only speculate as to the identity of the kings. If the kings or wise men really did come from Saba, they would certainly have used the Nabatean trade routes on which gold, incense and myrrh were transported, and which they brought as gifts for the Jesus child. Even if they came from Babylonia or Persia as some traditions say, they passed through the Nabatean kingdom on their journey. It is not impossible that one of the three kings was Aretas IV, who continued to maintain contact with Jerusalem and the Temple in later years.

In later Christian religious ceremonies, incense symbolized the link between the spiritual and the temporal world. When the resin is burned, it unfolds is characteristic features, and whose scent is not released until it begins to burn. The Sabean mysteries were *Phoenix mysteries,* which is also pointed out by von Gleich.[50] The phoenix is a mythical bird which is burned up in the fire and rises again from its ashes. There is a clear relationship here with the Christian concept of

Figure 17. Date palm, vine and bird, fourth to fifth century AD, approx. 72 x 30 cm, Shivta.

resurrection. A further symbol for the resurrection can be seen in the image of the date palm which is almost the only tree in the desert to bear fruit. The botanical name of this palm is *Phoenix dactylifera.* Because of its vitality, it was honoured in the ancient civilizations of the Orient as a symbol of the sun, and in Saba as a symbol of the God Attar; for the Nabateans it symbolized Dushrat.

The Christianity which developed in the Negev and other parts originally inhabited by the Nabateans, focused less on the death on the cross and more on the concept of the resurrection — the birth of the divine in human beings as Paul had experienced it in his spiritual vision at the gates of Damascus. Symbols in which we can recognize — the phoenix (also often represented as a peacock), the date palm and incense — therefore dominated Nabatean culture down to the level of the ornaments found in churches in the Negev (Figure 17).

Characteristics of early Christianity in the Negev

According to written church history, Christianity was introduced to the Negev in the middle of the fourth century. Rather than concentrate on historical accuracy, the Church chronicles were more concerned in making the development of Christianity fit in with the later veneration of the saints and the martyrs. A clear distinction was to be made with the *heathens* or *Saracens* (Arabs who had not yet embraced Christianity). A description by St Jerome, which he wrote down about 390 in Bethlehem, reports in a wonderful way on the role of St Hilarion in the Christianization of Elusa:

> The journey which he [Hilarion] once undertook in the desert Kadesh in order to visit his pupils. He reached Elusa with a great following of monks, and this happened on the day on which all the people had gathered in the temple of Venus for the annual festival. This goddess is venerated in the name of Lucifer, whom the Saracens worship. When it became known that Hilarion was journeying by (he had recently healed many Saracens possessed by demons), they went to welcome him ...,
> bowed their heads and called in the Syrian [Nabatean] language 'Barech,' i.e. 'Bless us.' He received them politely and modestly and prayed that they should serve God and not the stone. Crying copiously, he looked up to heaven and promised that if they believed in Christ he would visit them often. Through the wonderful mercy of God he did not leave them until they had drawn the plan of a church and their priest had been given a wreath with the symbol of Christ.[51]

This is the oldest document to report the conversion to Christianity in the Negev. The depiction of the event is clearly intended to show the heathen world as inferior, but from our perspective, there are nevertheless a number of important aspects. There was a temple to Venus, that is a star cult, in Elusa as late as the fourth century. Lucifer, the bearer of light, was also worshipped. Hilarion, who as a Christian monk must have been well known to the local population, left the priest of Venus in his original office, after having given him the symbol of Christ. The conversion to Christianity is presented here as an absolutely harmonious process, a continuation of the religious customs which had existed for centuries. Only by these means could Hilarion's appearance lead to the mass conversion as described by Jerome.

As soon as Constantine began to tolerate and recognize the Christian religion, the construction of churches started everywhere in the Negev, in Mampsis, Elusa, Ruheiba, Avdat and Shivta. This would not have happened in such a far-flung corner of the Roman empire, far from the centres of Christian belief, if a sufficient number of Christians did not already live there.

The churches represented more than a gathering place for the early Christians in the Negev. Baptism at that time must be understood as an initiation into the Christian mysteries. Acceptance into the community was then still linked with the condition that the person concerned had already been baptized. Many fonts, particularly those in Shivta, Avdat and Mampsis, are of a size which clearly indicates that they were meant for adults (Figure 60). The person to be baptized was immersed in the basin and, through a separation into the elements of his being, experienced a state akin to death. Ritual baptism was an event which connected him with the life of Christ. Admission to the congregation was thus accompanied by a type of crossing the threshold. Celebration of the sacraments could only be experienced as a mystical act if it had been preceded by such a preparation.

The first churches in the Negev were still relatively small inside and only had one apse, but were soon extended to three aisles and were given two additional apses. Six pillars in two parallel rows divided the space into seven transverse bays. This meant that the walk to the alter was divided into seven sections (for a detailed description of the churches of Shivta, see p. 196). The space was dark, lit only by a few candles and the pale daylight entered through the tiny windows (see Figure 18). The experience of the transition from the external world into the interior space of the church is illustrated in the following words by Rudolf Steiner:

> When a man looks at nature his gaze is ... going into infinity,
> never reaching an end ... But the gaze is bounded and
> completed when one faces a work of great architecture created
> with the aim of intercepting the vision, rescuing it from the
> pull of nature.[52]

Figure 18. Reconstruction attempt of the Northern Church in Shivta according to the ideas of the Colt expedition. Although the drawing diverges in some of the details from the actual architecture, it nevertheless manages to transmit something of the original impression of the space.

98

The people of the Negev were surrounded by a barren environment without any vegetation worth mentioning. The landscape was open to the gaze in all directions and there was nothing to stop it penetrating to the horizon. The round spheres of the three apses, which arrested and focused the look of those participating in the religious ceremony, are a prime example of this 'intercepting the vision' which the desert threatened to pull away (see Figure 65).

The church with three apses originates in the Negev.[53] In the fifth and sixth centuries, the dead began to be buried in the courtyard of the church. Whereas in Europe only members of the priesthood or the ruling class were buried within the precincts of the church, here ordinary believers too were put to rest near the alter. This is indicative of special community structures. The early cult of the dead, the attention paid to the soul of the deceased, was now given a new significance. Christianity produced a state of soul in people through which they could find access to the divine world through their own inner experience. This meant that there was an intimate link with individuals who operated as Church fathers at the very beginning of Christianity. It was on the basis of this attitude that the cult of keeping reliquaries developed. Stone containers for reliquaries were often kept in side apses of churches. Urns similar to the ones which were placed symbolically on the top of monuments to the dead in Petra (see Figure 45) now entered the sacred area of the church where the congregation could walk past them in connection with the celebration of the sacraments.

If at the time of the Roman emperor Trajan the Negev had served primarily as a corridor between Arabia and the Mediterranean, with the most important trade routes running through it, economically it had now become largely independent. Agriculture and wine growing in particular became the main sources of income for the region. An indigenous Christian religion also developed, including the development of a kind of monastic system. In various places such as Shivta and Ruheiba monasteries arose which were at first built outside existing settlements, but which then became agricultural centres and attracted many new settlers in their own right.

Early Christianity and Manicheism

The gnostic stream had its origin in the teachings of Mani, born in 216 in Mesopotamia. Gnosticism also influenced early Christianity, had many followers particularly in the eastern Mediterranean area and is likely to have influenced the Nabatean region as well. As late as the eighth century it spread beyond the frontiers of the Roman empire, before being eradicated by the institutions of the Church. Although forms of Manichean monasticism and asceticism entered the Christian tradition, Manicheism was vigorously opposed by the Church.[54] One of its most bitter opponents was Titus, the fourth-century bishop of Bostra, a Nabatean city in the North (now called Bosra). The polemics of Titus against the Manicheans, composed partly in the Syrian-Nabatean language, would probably never have been written if there had not been so many Gnostics in his diocese.

Nevertheless, in the early stages of Christianity, the Church had a tendency to beatify figures who had great prestige and many followers, without accepting those elements of their belief which did not accord with official Church teachings, and which the Church considered to be heresy.

In Nessana, one of the flourishing cities of the province which had meanwhile been given the official name *Palaestina Salutaris,* a large number of papyrus scrolls dating from the fifth to the seventh century was discovered during excavations in the 1930s. They provide important information about the life of the Nabateans in the Negev during the Byzantine age. One of the scrolls describes the deeds of St George in a way which bears an astonishing resemblance to the life of Mani as it is traditionally told. George, a young and wealthy nobleman, resisted the anti-Christian Roman laws. He was killed three times only to be resurrected three times. In the end he was imprisoned in the house of a widow. There he performed numerous miracles. He made a dead branch blossom, brought a dead ox back to life, healed the son of the widow of his blindness and brought the dead back to life.[55]

The papyrus from Nessana survived church censorship, which

had a single image of the saints as its objective. The description of the life of St George which it contains is one of the oldest in existence. The motif of the Vanquisher of the Dragon does not appear in Europe until as late as the twelfth century. Only a few of the many ancient acts of St George contain the episode with the widow and the miracles of the resurrection. The motifs of the resurrection and his command over life forces place him close to the Nabatean form of Christianity. The cult of St George was widespread in the Negev. There is a monastery dedicated to St George near Shivta (see p. 217). The extent to which gnostic-Manichean thought influenced the religious views of the inhabitants of the Negev must remain unanswered given the existing lack of documentation from this time. However, the Nabatean region and its civilization does appear to have provided fertile ground for a variety of syncretic forms even in the Christian era.

Christianity spread rapidly among the Nabateans. Since it appeared as a continuation of existing religious faiths, this transition was free of any revolutionary incisions. We know of no sources which speak of the violent conversion of the inhabitants of the Negev. The bishop of Eila (present-day Eilat) took part in the Council of Nicea as early as 325. Elusa, on the other hand, had not at this time converted *en masse* to Christianity. A bishop by the name of Abdallah (undoubtedly an Arabic Nabatean name) from Elusa was not present until the church council of Ephesus (431). The bishops of Petra were among the participants at the synods of Sardica (342) and Seleucia (359). The fact that one of these Arabic bishops had the name Aretas leaves no doubt about his origins. Paganism appears to have co-existed with Christianity until the start of the fifth century. It was quite possible to be a Christian and still believe in other spiritual beings and make sacrifices to them. The old gods were only gradually forgotten.

Nabatean Christianity now experienced a brief renaissance. Increasing emigration and the spread of Islam soon put an end to it. For a time the two religions continued to co-exist in peace. In Shivta, a mosque was built next to the Southern Church, but approximately two hundred years after the Muslims penetrated the Negev the words of the Christian sacrament were silenced completely. The wheel of history turned back by 1500 years. Only a few nomads roamed the plains and mountains. Former agricultural land reverted to infertile desert whose silence continues to leave the questions of today's researchers unanswered.

CHAPTER FOUR

The Language of Nabatean Art

If we wish to develop an understanding of classical art, in which individual currents are only expressed to a limited degree, this can only
be achieved in connection with a study of the lifestyle of ancient peoples and their spiritual background. Michael Avi-Yonah, one of the pioneers in the research of classical works of art in the Holy Land,
points out that the art of the Nabateans is far removed from the art of
a desert people.[1] He notes that its unique character can only be uncovered by taking into account the particular social structures without
which the co-existence of people of various backgrounds under the
most difficult conditions, would not have been possible.

For example, whereas Greek art produced unique stylistic characteristics which are clearly distinguished from those of other cultures,
no such comparable stylistic independence is evident in Nabatean art.
Its nature is not revealed in its individual characteristics but only in
the overall effect of its creations.

Early art of the nomadic period

Sources remain silent about Nabatean art during the early nomadic
period. We can assume that at a time when Nabatean tribes roamed
through the desert looking for water and fresh fruit for their herds,
completely immersed in their shepherd existence, artistic creation
was expressed mostly on a linguistic level, in the telling of events that
actually happened, or relating to inner experiences, as is still the case
with the nomads today. News passed on by word of mouth, sagas and

stories filled the hours spent communally when all the duties of the day had been done. Craft tools were made exclusively for everyday use. A nomadic culture is restricted to the bare necessities and avoids unnecessary household goods which have to be packed and transported from one place to another on the backs of camels. For the same reason ceramic vessels were not used — or only those which were not fired and thus not easily broken.

In the civilizations of the classical world, artistic creation was seen as a repetition of the divine act of creation through human activity. This made all types of art sacred; secular trends were unable to gain a foothold because people were deeply religious. The works of art show in characteristic fashion the way in which the physical world, imbued with the spirit of God, was experienced by the people of that time. Even a superficial inspection of Nabatean artistic creation clearly shows that it was governed by a non-figurative tendency. Only in later stages, after the birth of Christ, were the gods depicted in human form; and even then such anthropomorphic depiction of the gods was restricted to the outer reaches of the kingdom where outside influences, particularly Greek, had come to dominate.

The development of temple architecture

The oldest finds which provide evidence of artistic activity among the Nabateans originate from the same period in which a taboo from the nomadic period, described by Diodorus, was broken and the construction of temples and buildings began. Nabatean architecture in particular, presents the academic world with a phenomenon which has not so far been given a satisfactory explanation. Whereas other civilizations required a certain amount of time for their architecture to mature, developing from primitive beginnings to ever higher levels of perfection, even the earliest Nabatean buildings occur in a fully developed form. The explanation that foreign architects were at work is not sufficient by itself.

Undoubtedly use was made of their technical and artistic skills, but the actual building impulse can only be explained on the basis of the

104

particular purpose which the architecture was meant to serve and which had its source in the Nabatean way of thinking.

Nabatean temples can be divided into two main types. In one, the inner sanctum is surrounded by an external wall which forms a single space; in the other, the interior space is divided into three. The largest temple in Petra, called *Qasr al-Bint Farun* (Castle of the Pharaoh's daughter), can be considered to be the synthesis of both types (Figure 16).

The Petran monuments to the dead

Nabatean art found its highest expression in the Petran monuments to the dead, and their ornamentation. These monuments can be classified from various perspectives, but in principle there are two main types which even the unschooled eye can distinguish when visiting Petra. The first includes façades with simple designs as well as free-standing monuments (Figures 42 and 51), the second comprises more magnificent rock monuments such as, for example, the Treasury, which has become a landmark of Nabatean art (Figure 19). On leaving the gorge which provides the sole access from the east to the former capital of the Nabateans, the visitor is faced directly by this almost forty metre high building, whose Arabic name, Al-Khasneh, means *Pharaoh's treasury*. It is not actually a building in the literal sense, but it might much more accurately be described as a *sculpture* hewn out of the rock.

The lower storey is crowned by a Hellenistic architrave which is supported by six pillars. Its interior consists of three rooms which are almost disappointingly small in relation to the magnificent façade. The upper storey is a mock façade which has an exclusively decorative and symbolic significance. While the architecture of the Treasury has been comprehensively investigated its purpose has still not been fully clarified. As we shall see later, there are many indications that it was a cult or mystery site used for the cult of the dead, but not as a mausoleum for their earthly remains but as a place where a link to the soul of the deceased was sought (see page 187). Such an interpretation would also accord with the symbolism of the façade:

Figure 19. The Treasury. First century BC, Petra.

the interior of the temple is not hidden behind the façade but is projected to the outside and appears in the particular features of the upper storey. The world of the dead is not reached by entering the interior of the building. It is positioned on a higher level; there are no further spaces behind the mock façade, and it cannot therefore be reached by physical means.

All the figurative depictions which decorate this monument have remained incomplete. A closer look shows that, contrary to views held in the past, the figures were not damaged in a later period. It is likely that work on the figurative part of the façade was stopped at the time that the figures were created or that they were disfigured immediately after their completion. A possible explanation for this curious procedure might be that Greek artists undertook the work who took little notice of the ban on the creation of images, and were forced by the Nabateans to break off their work in its half-finished state. Avraham Negev described the selective destruction of these monuments as Nabatean iconoclasm.[2] A fully sculpted depiction of the human form in a memorial for the dead would have been akin to blasphemy to Nabatean thinking. It would have been wholly inappropriate for the soul of a dead person, just loosening its bonds with the material and form world in order to rise to the divine spheres, to encounter such images in ritual surroundings. The rock monuments of Petra in particular provide evidence that the absence of figurative images in Nabatean art has nothing to do with a lack of ability in the artists.

The start of a new era

Rabel II, the last king in the line of Nabatean rulers, is given the title *Soter,* that is *Saviour,* in many inscriptions, or described as 'Rabel, King of the Nabateans who revived and redeemed his people.' We do not know what services he performed to acquire such an honourable title. Avraham Negev suspects that it was under the reign of Rabel II that the Nabateans fully abandoned their nomadic lifestyle and that it was he who led them out of an economic recession and brought them renewed prosperity through radical reform.[3] This revival and saving of his people was also reflected in Nabatean art, which enjoyed a renewed flowering.

But the impulses which resulted from his rule appear to have had their greatest significance in the field of *social* creativity. In his thirty-six years in office, he ensured that the last remnants of ethnic-nationalist tendencies disappeared. Old conventions were adapted to the requirements of the times. Thus the freedom which the Nabateans prized above all else, and which was deeply rooted in their ancient nomadic traditions, was preserved by renouncing their national and political independence and subjecting themselves to foreign rule. In AD 106, the year when Rabel II died, Nabatea became a Roman province. The new kind of freedom under *Pax Romana* allowed the Nabateans to preserve peace and develop their own culture, and lasted for five hundred years.

The development of domestic architecture

The kingdom of Nabatea was finished as a kingdom, but a truly royal period was just beginning in the fields of art and architecture. The construction of domestic houses began during the reign of the last king, Rabel II. Many people now lived in permanent stone dwellings. Here too, there is no sign of gradual development. The people left their camel skin tents to move into houses whose mature architecture could stand comparison with other building traditions in the classical world. Today, it is impossible to determine its origins with any certainty. With the irrigation systems, in contrast, it is possible to show an affinity with methods which were used in ancient Saba. However, so far there have been no studies comparing possible links between Sabean and Nabatean domestic architecture.

Nabatean dwellings were investigated in Avdat (Oboda), Mampsis (Mamshit, Kurnub) and other cities in the Negev. In Petra, too, research has led to valuable findings about Nabatean architecture, but most buildings from the early period of domestic architecture lie buried under ruins from the Byzantine period. Although many of the later buildings show improvements in relation to older dwellings constructed around the time of Christ, we can summarize that there were no significant changes in Nabatean architecture from the time of its first appearance.

Nabatean dwellings had up to three storeys and reached a maximum height of twelve metres. The walls were eighty centimetres thick and consisted of three separate layers: an outer one made of hard rock with a smoothed surface, an inner one made of rough stone for the better adherence of mortar, and the cavity in between the two which was filled with smaller stones and earth. This provided walls with good insulation which kept the interior cool in the summer and warm in the winter. The lower storeys were made of a particularly hard stone, the upper ones of a softer material. In Shivta in particular, a settlement which has been relatively well preserved, we can see buildings whose second storey is still preserved.

The absence of wood as a building material ensured that advanced techniques of arch construction were developed. Each room was vaulted by several arches which carried a roof made of stone slabs (Figures 20 and 25). The distance between the individual arches was determined by the size of these slabs which were made from stone materials available in the immediate environment. The harder the stone, the longer the slabs, which meant that the distance between the arches could be increased.

Many doorposts were decorated. The threshold, which was crossed on entering the house was tapered at both ends; the doorposts were given a similar shape thus imitating the contours of the human body. This created an awareness of crossing the threshold. While European Medieval buildings had low doors indicating that most people of the time were smaller in stature than those of the twentieth century (an impression confirmed by the size of knights' armour), it comes as a surprise that the entrances to the rooms of Nabatean houses were 180 cm high or more. If we assume that this was so not only for aesthetic reasons, we may conclude that the people living here were of imposing stature.[4]

Some houses had inner courtyards which were surrounded by individual living quarters. The windows were small and were situated just below the ceiling. This allowed the smoke to leave while preventing direct sunlight to enter in the summer. Typical and unique

Figure 20. Attempt at a partial reconstruction of a domestic building near the Southern Church of Shivta (after A. Segal).

features of Nabatean architecture were stair towers by which the upper storeys were reached. The remains of stone water pipes can often still be found in the ruins. In the winter these channelled the water from the roof into cisterns belonging to each house and in the summer they were used to top up the cisterns with water brought by camel or donkey (Figure 21).

110

Figure 21. Cistern in a house in Shivta. The rain water was channelled from the roof into the approx. 3 to 4 m deep cistern by means of a pipe.

Ceramics and other items of practical use

At the time that permanent dwellings began to be built, we encounter remarkable achievements in the crafts field in the manufacture of pottery products. Finds uncovered in excavations bear the unmistakable characteristics of Nabatean art, and are unique in terms of quality providing evidence of tremendous craft skills.

In 1959, Avraham Negev discovered a potter's workshop in Avdat. This showed that the earliest pottery of this type originated in the second half of the last century BC, and that production of such earthenware occurred within a period of about one century. Earlier theories which dated such findings to the third century BC are thus considered to have been superseded.[5] The noteworthy feature of

111

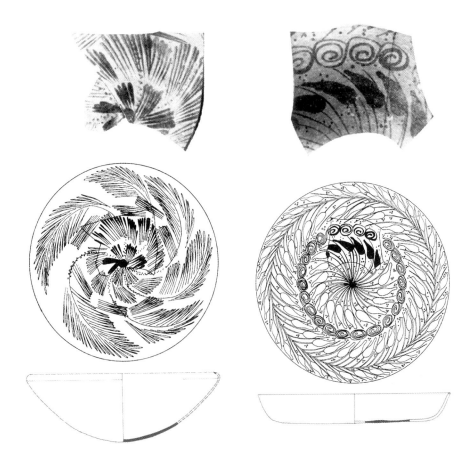

Figure 22. Spiral rosette on the fragment of a clay dish, Avdat.

Nabatean earthenware is the delicacy of the bowls and plates. Their sides were often no more than one or two millimetres thick. Production of large quantities of such eggshell ceramics required a very high technical standard. It is no longer possible to tell whether it was Nabateans or foreign masters who worked in this field, but the stylistic and craft characteristics of these products, which also includes the unmistakable ornamentation (Figures 22 and 23), were restricted to the Nabatean region. Nowhere in the whole of the Middle East and the Mediterranean area were ceramics of comparable beauty produced.

    If we look at sites where larger quantities of this earthenware were

112

Figure 23. Painted Nabatean dish with palmettes, figs and olives.

found, it is striking that they were mostly religious sites such as the acropolis of Avdat and the theatres of Petra and Elusa. The bowls which were found there are relatively small, have a diameter of about seven centimetres, an almost semi-circular shape and no flat surface for putting them down; they had to be held in the hand and could not be placed on a table. Such vessels were used for religious meals and are of particular delicacy. It may be that they were only meant to be used only once.

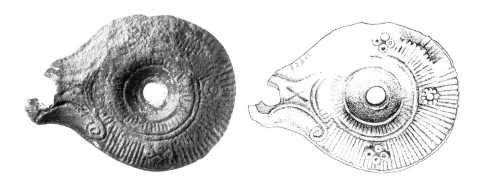

Figure 24. Typical Nabatean oil lamp with radiating decoration.

The painting of these clay vessels is also characteristic. The decoration consisting of fine lines recalls plant forms and is intended to express growth and the power of germination (Figure 23). Human forms or depictions of animals are missing completely, another indication of the non-figurative tendency in Nabatean art. Some patterns also resemble fine crystallization patterns as found with copper chloride, or frost on windows. In his typological investigation, Karl Schmitt-Korte divides the patterns into decorative schemes and distinguishes main groups in the predominant basic motifs.[6] We encounter the same motifs in transformation in architectural ornamentation and sill decorations (Figures 29 and 30) in the churches of the Negev which were built at the end of the fourth century and later. The Nabateans also developed their own style in the production of oil lamps (Figure 24). The ray-like patterns with rings make them typical representatives of Nabatean culture.

The Christian basilica

When the first churches were built in the Negev, the Nabateans were already living in permanent settlements. Nomads still ranged through the desert with their herds but their numbers were getting smaller. Hundreds of farmers established themselves in the areas surrounding the settlements, tending their land and working the dry, furrowed

114

desert soil. The constant effort of making the desert bloom, the hard existence of both the rural and urban population, which was constantly concerned with preserving the basis of its existence, produced a special sort of person. Ways of life and the requirements connected with life in the desert also came to expression in the religious field, not least in the form given to ritual spaces. The churches in the Negev not only belong to the oldest Christian buildings, they show clear characteristics of a separate development.

It is not clear who the architects of these churches were. In a letter to the Consul of the Province of Pontus, the Roman emperor Trajan wrote: 'You will have no shortage of architects. There is no province in which capable *ingeniosos homines* could not be found.'[7] That referred to men of *genius*. It is probably the earliest use of this term in the meaning of engineer. However, the religious buildings of the classical world are not only the result of highly developed architectural and technical skills, they also show an intuitive empathy which created buildings which were in harmony with, and enhanced, the religious content and practices.[8] (Freemasonry originally continued this tradition of building which enhanced religious aspirations.)

In Shivta there is a special atmosphere which can be sensed when contemplating the semi-circular apses of the churches which remain standing to their full height (see Figures 53 and 59). Avraham Negev, who devoted his life to the investigation of Nabatean culture, regretfully admitted with resignation in a conversation in 1993: 'Church architecture in the Negev speaks a special language. I do not understand it.' Something which has remained hidden even to the most well-informed person in this field can only be guessed at. It is the language which may appear incomprehensible to the present day observer, but whose beautiful sound can still be clearly heard.

Ornamentation

From the beginning, the architecture of the cities of the Negev showed evidence of a high level of skill. The contrast between the magnificent architecture and, the relatively modest decoration of the buildings, particularly the churches, is therefore all the more

Figure 25. Arches of a domestic building with some of the roof preserved. Shivta.

surprising. Many city inhabitants and members of the rural population in surrounding areas could not read or write.[9] An added difficulty was that three different languages were in use at the time, Nabatean, Greek and increasingly Latin. The universal language which spoke to the feelings of people consisted of images and symbols. On entering the church, the visitor encountered whole sequences of pictures in the form of reliefs. Several rosettes of various types could be found on the door lintels of religious and other buildings (Figures 29 and 30). There can be no doubt that they too had special meaning. They were intended to produce a transformation in the soul of the observer on entering the religious space.

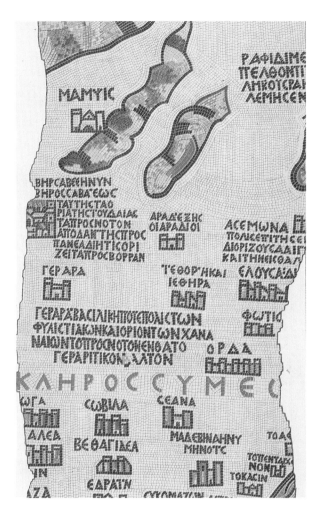

Figure 26. Part of the sixth-century Madaba mosaic map showing Mampsis (top left) and Elusa (right).

Like the buildings themselves, the ornamentation of the churches also had its origins in the fourth century. Two hundred years had passed since the last production of classical Nabatean pottery. One reason for this might have been connected with Christianization. Previously, ceramic vessels had been used mainly for religious purposes. In Christian times, however, ceremonial banquets for the dead were no longer held. Burial rites changed as the concept of resurrection took hold in early Christianity.[10] The Eucharist with the transubstantiation of bread and wine replaced the ancient Nabatean religious ceremonies. The profusion of ceramic products as had been manufactured in the past were no longer used for this, but the motifs which were used on these products were now encountered as rosettes above the church portals.

Purely ornamental motifs were now also joined by some figurative representations, mostly bird shapes. The dove, an ancient image of the human soul, became a symbol of the Holy Spirit in Christianity. The peacock, spreading his feathers, indicated the ability of humans to extend their consciousness into the supersensory realm. The date palm, also known as the phoenix tree, represented the conquest over death as well as the principle of fertility applied to the spiritual realm. Another frequently depicted motif was the fish, and dolphins in particular. The latter live in water as a mammal but can rise above it for brief periods of time. This invites comparison with the human situation: as spiritual beings in origin, humans live in the physical world as if in a foreign element; but through the power of Christian belief they can rise to the heights of the spiritual world. In Khirbet et-Tannur, east of the Dead Sea, depictions of the gods have been found surrounded by dolphins.[11]

In Shivta, there is a capital depicting a bird which looks neither like a dove nor a peacock (Figure 27). It is drinking out of a goblet and is surrounded by flame like shapes on both sides. It is a depiction of the phoenix. It rises from the flames within the circle of the sun and its resurrection is due to the sacrament being presented in the chalice.

In addition to such figurative decorations, there are also many plant motifs on capitals and other building elements. Fertility and the power of growth in nature remained a dominant theme. The economy with which these symbols was used must have made their effect all the stronger.

Ornamental art in Nabatean churches

In order to gain a clearer understanding of Nabatean ornamental art, we shall digress to an alien culture whose influence has already been mentioned (pp. 63 and 87). There can be no doubt that the Nabateans, as caravan traders, reached India.[12] They returned not just with material trade goods but also with a wealth of spiritual ideas.

Figure 27. Bird with chalice decorating a capital, Shivta (lost).

Even within Jewish culture, where an effort was made to limit the influence of outside thinking, a knowledge existed of Indian religion and mysticism. When the last bulwark of the Jewish revolution against the Romans, the fortress of Massada on the Dead Sea, was about to fall, the leader of the Jews, Eleazar Ben Ja'ir, saw the only way out as the mass suicide of the approximately two thousand people who had fled there. He preferred to live as a free man in the realm of the dead rather than as a slave under the Romans. In doing so, he referred to the example of the Indians and their religious conviction. Josephus quotes his words:

> And if we look for true witnesses among the foreigners, let us look at the ways of the people of India who devote their whole life to wisdom. These wise people bear their life without joy since their existence appears to them like a punishment of

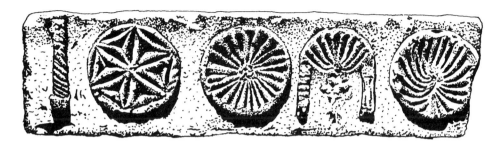

Figure 29. Beam with rosettes, 110 x 30 cm, Shivta.

heaven and it is their desire to liberate the soul from the imprisonment of the body.[13]

In the sixth century before Christ, at the same time as the Nabateans are thought to have settled in the Negev, in India Buddha taught a new path of knowledge by which human beings could achieve a vision of the supersensory. At each stage of knowledge they were enabled to activate the chakras organs which perceive the supersensory. This comes to symbolic expression in the wheel of the sun motif which also appears on Nabatean pottery in the first century AD (see Figure 22), and in Nabatean churches in the fourth century (see Figures 29 and 30).[14]

Plain rosettes can be recognized on many entablatures on monuments in Petra which in that form were still *blind* or, rather *silent* (Figures 28 and 45). They returned in changed form above the entrances to churches and began to *speak* (Figures 29 and 30). There the rosettes (in groups of three or four) are decorated, and could also be described as seals. As well as animal shapes, which are depicted between the seals and also above or below them, there are frequent depictions of the vine. This is a clear sign of the radical transformation of the Nabatean view of the world. Its symbolic significance in Christianity needs no further explanation. If drinking wine had previously

Figure 28. 'Silent rosettes,' rosettes above the architrave of the Monastery (Ed-Deir), Petra.

Figure 30. Beam above the entrance to the Southern Church in Shivta. The original was destroyed by vandalism in 1995.

been a criminal offence, it was now the focus of religious practice. In most cases, the first rosette from the left depicts a leaf motif (Figure 30). Six leaves are in a state of rest. The six-leafed rosette is a variation of the Christ monogram, but it can also be considered as a symbol of the element which in Indian tradition was described as the *chakras* or *Lotus flower* and which enabled perception of the supersensory.[15] The middle emblem depicts the Cross surrounded by the orb of the sun, with the letters Alpha and Omega — beginning and end — alongside. To the right there is a rosette in the shape of a spiral whose leaves appear to turn. All three rosettes are linked by a band in lemniscate form.

Another sequence of such seals starts to the left with a column (Figure 29). It symbolizes the human being standing upright. This is followed by a rosette at rest, followed by a second one with greater differentiation. To the right of that there is an arch with a Cross underneath which was presumably damaged at a later time. It is concluded by a spiral rosette.

This sequence of motifs is repeated in a similar fashion in other depictions as well: a leaf motif at rest is transformed into a spiral rosette. What does this sequence of images tell the observer? It is as if these symbols at the threshold of the church call out:

... You approach the altar, the sacrament. The process which takes place here as transubstantiation occurs on the level of the life forces with which we have been connected for centuries and which are depicted on the religious vessels of our ancestors. There are forces in nature which we have learned to control and which enable us to live in the desert. You are approaching the sacrament; you do not yet look into the spirit realm as our ancestors did. Now proceed through the Christian ritual! The Lord will awaken your sense of the spirit through which you will recognize him.

Perhaps sentiments such as these were roused deep in the soul by the symbols above the church entrances. In this way art stood in the service of *religio,* the re-connection of human beings with their spiritual origins.

CHAPTER FIVE

From Nomads to Farmers

The development within a few centuries, of a relatively small nomadic tribe living in an inhospitable environment like the Negev, into
one of the most prosperous peoples of antiquity is no less of a riddle
than the achievements in the cultural realm, of which there are so
many in Nabatean history. One of the most important reasons for such
prosperity is likely to lie in the development of a purely *peace economy*. The Nabateans hated waging war and all that accompanied it.
Although they maintained a well-trained army, they only used it in
emergencies and always attempted to avoid military conflict.

The desert environment

Even the earliest mention of the Nabateans, in the description by
Diodorus from 312 BC (see p. 47), provides valuable information
about the economic circumstances of the Nabateans:

> Some Nabateans rear camels while others rear sheep which
> graze in the desert. The Nabateans are probably the wealthiest
> among all the Arabic shepherd tribes even if they number no
> more than ten thousand. Many of them transport expensive
> spices, myrrh and incense from *Arabia Eudaemon* to the sea
> coast.[1]

This is followed by a description of the equipment which was used
to dig cisterns and camouflage them. Strabo mentions that there were

no horses in the whole of the country. Camels were used for riding and as beasts of burden.[2] This was to change later. Diodorus' report continues:

> They water their herds every third day so that they do not
> constantly require water in areas where there is none and if
> they have to flee. Their food consists of milk and meat and also
> the plants which grow wild there. For pepper grows there and
> on trees much so-called tree honey which they drink mixed
> with water.

The herds supplied that necessities of daily life, food, and the materials to produce clothing and tents. There are several oases on the shores of the Dead Sea. *Tree honey* was won from the fruits of the date palm which grows wild there.

The whole development of Nabatean culture was influenced by the desert. In all cases where civilizations have achieved a high level of material prosperity, there has been a long period of settled life and it is accompanied by a gradual maturing over time. However, this was not the case with the Nabateans: here a tribal community largely preserved its tribal traditions and yet managed to achieve a level of prosperity which was referred to more than once in classical history. In contrast to other peoples, wealth did not lead to spiritual decadence. Supported by a flourishing economy, it was possible for their civilization to truly flower. Not only was the transformation of the desert into fertile agricultural land one of the pillars of their material prosperity, without which a highly developed civilization could not have arisen in this environment. It also provided the basis for the development of one of its basic motifs — the production of *life* as the highest form of art.

Incense, myrrh, asphalt: Nabatean wealth

In his description of the attempts by the successors of Alexander the Great to incorporate the country of the Nabateans into the Greek empire, Diodorus adds a description of the Dead Sea, where he mentions

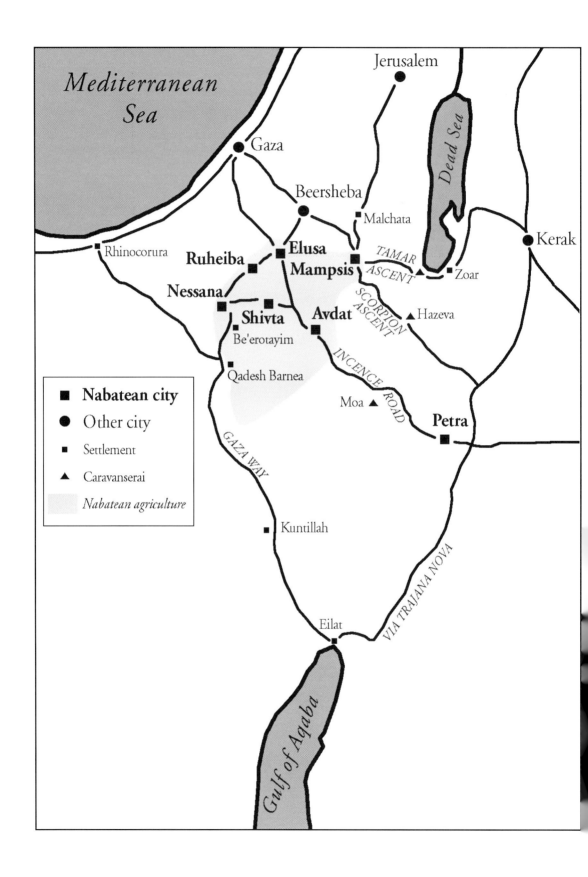

Figure 31. Clay horse's head, Avdat.

asphalt which periodically rises from the depths. The Nabateans used three-man rafts to recover it.

> The Barbarians [for this is what the Nabateans are called here] derive income from pitch out of the earth by exporting it to Egypt where it is bought to mummify the dead; for if it is not added to the aromatic substances, bodies will not be preserved.[3]

These few indications supplement our picture of the early Nabatean period. Three substances produced both material and spiritual wealth: asphalt, which was recovered from the Dead Sea, incense and myrrh. All these substances are used where life and death meet at the threshold to the spiritual world. Paradoxically, it was the Nabateans, characterized by extraordinary vitality, who became the main suppliers in the whole of the classical world of substances required for the cult of the dead. Corpses in Egypt could not be embalmed without asphalt from the Dead Sea. Incense and myrrh were sacramental substances which from ancient times accompanied the rise of human prayers to the divine on the altars of ancient civilizations. It was only with the increasing decadence of Roman civilization that they also served to satisfy profane needs which grew out of luxury and excess. They were made into cosmetic products used in baths. Just as the decline of Roman civilization led to the debasing if

Map 2. Nabatean trade routes and settlements in Roman times.   127

the triclinia, the Roman thermal complexes were institutions whose origins lie in religious baptism.

Incense *(Boswellia carteri)* and myrrh *(Commiphora abyssinica),* are obtained from plants native to southern Arabia. Incisions are cut in their branches to produce a sap which thickens to resin in the air. The ethereal oils it contains are released on heating and produce the typical scent. The deeply religious attitude which accompanied the cultivation of these plants can be seen in Pliny's description of how these substances are won.[4] The main area of cultivation of these plants in Saba at the time was called *Scariba.* Pliny tells us the significance of that name: *hoc significare Graeci mysterium dicunt* — 'which according to the Greeks means "mystery".'

Only three thousand families were permitted to cultivate the precious resin and trade in it. These rights were always passed from one generation to the next. The harvest took place twice a year. During harvesting, they were not allowed to enter the company of women or to take part in burial ceremonies. The cultivation and processing of these substances had a sacred religious meaning to the Sabeans. The incense was brought from the fields into the capital by a special gate where one tenth of the goods was handed over to the priests. Before that it was not allowed to be traded. According to some reports, the incense in the forests was communal property and the annual income was distributed among the population. The forests always remained unguarded and no thief would have dared to use these valuable resins for his own profit. Circumstances at the other end of the incense road, in Alexandria, were completely different. Here there could never be enough guards to secure the warehouses.

The caravan trade and its organization

Pliny does not expressly mention the Nabateans as traders who transported myrrh and incense to the Mediterranean ports. His reports refer exclusively to the harvesting of resin. And yet in his *Natural History* we find very illuminating remarks relating to the Nabateans. The route from Thomna in the land of the Gebbites on the edge of Saba, where the actual caravan route began, was divided into sixty-five daily stages (see Map 5). A caravan could managed the distance from southern Arabia to the Mediterranean in nine to ten weeks. Many of these caravans undertook their journeys after the harvest. There were stops one day's travel apart where people and animals could spend the night. Pliny quotes the costs which had to be paid en route for water, food and accommodation. He also puts a figure the value of the goods which were transported. The price per pound for incense must have been three, five or six dinars depending on its quality. Myrrh was traded at between three and fifty dinars. A camel weighing between 350 and 600 kilograms can carry a load of up to 300 kilograms.[5] A caravan of fifty camels could thus transport goods with a total value of up to one million dinars. Cargo of such high value had of course to be strictly guarded. Not only were caravanserais set up, a special force was also set up with the purpose of guarding the trade routes.

Camels are the ideal beasts of burden in the desert. They can subsist on very little and do not need water during the winter since the moisture in the grass is sufficient. They do not mind high temperatures and can travel routes without difficulty which would be inaccessible for donkeys or horses. It is likely that the caravanserais which Pliny mentions, some of which have been found in archeological excavations, were also used for camel breeding, for active trade required a sufficient supply of beasts of burden. Camel breeding is thus likely to have been a further important economic factor in the life of the Nabateans.

The caravan trade and the religious importance of cultivating incense and myrrh in southern Arabia may have been the reasons why increasing numbers of emigrants from Saba gradually settled along the caravan route. They may have been the pioneers of Nabatean culture in the Negev. After the destruction of the Temple of Jerusalem in 586 BC, there was a temporary drop in the demand for myrrh and incense, but the spread of Greek civilization in the fourth century BC reopened these markets, and strong demand for these precious substances developed in the whole of the classical world.

The beginnings of settlement

Maintaining the connection with the home of their ancestors, something to which there were economic but also religious and spiritual aspects, may have been a decisive incentive for the Nabateans to adhere to their nomadic existence into the first century BC. The settlement process only began once considerable wealth had spread throughout the population. The Romans acquired incense and myrrh for largely secular reasons. This resulted in a rise in demand which could have meant an enormous increase in turnover for the Nabateans, but developments took a different course. In 108 AD, immediately after the death of the Nabatean king Rabel II, the Roman Emperor Trajan had a new trade route built, the Via Traiana Nova (see Map 3). Now the most important trade route no longer went through the Negev but took the longer way through the Jordanian mountains.

This is often seen as the real reason why the Nabateans gave up the caravan trade and turned to other activities. But if we look at the numerous anomalies in Nabatean culture this explanation appears too simple. We will therefore consider another possibility. By using incense and myrrh for cosmetic purposes, the Romans ignored the religious and spiritual significance which the Nabateans accorded these substances. The people who preserved myrrh and incense exclusively for religious purposes against the background of ancient traditions must have considered what they would have thought of as the blasphemous use of these substances as an unforgivable sacrilege. It is possible that they might have refused to continue supplying them for this reason, and that they withdrew from the trade. If we assume such a boycott, the Romans would indeed have been forced to build up their own trade circumventing the Nabatean region in order to cover their continuously growing demand.

The Nabatean economy experienced a clear slump during this period in the first century AD. This can be seen in particular from the silver content of their coinage. In the second half of the first century it sank to twenty per cent. This is the lowest content of precious metal in coins in the history of Nabatean minting, and is a reliable indicator of the prevailing economic situation.[6]

Christianity and its importance for the economy

The more Christianity spread, and the more people came into contact with it, the more a new trait of the Nabateans began to emerge. It might be described as a more *mature* attitude to the earth. Taking possession of the land, the establishment of permanent settlements and the associated settled way of life are the clearest indications of this. Permanent building materials began to be used; houses were built of stone. Agriculture was developed and horse breeding began.

According to Strabo's report, there were still no horses in the Nabatean region in the first century BC, but now horse breeding began on a significant scale.[7] Stables can still be seen today (Figure 32). Aerial photos of Avdat show a crater-like shape in the north-east of the city. Avraham Negev interpreted this as an arena which was used for training horses. The Arab thoroughbreds which are still valued today go back to Nabatean breeders.[8] Such a mature attitude to the earth has both a literal and metaphorical meaning in this context. Horses have always become the companions of human beings in ancient civilizations when a certain maturity in relation to the latter's existence on earth has been also achieved. With the Nabateans, horse breeding became a central economic factor from the first century onwards and remained so until the end of their civilization.

The flowering of agriculture and irrigation

In the first century AD, the Nabateans completely gave up their nomadic existence and centuries-old traditions. Hitherto building, planting and drinking wine had been punishable crimes; but now suddenly the desert was made fertile. With this step, too, the Nabatean anomaly which we have already encountered appears again: a new, unexpected cultural phase produced a highly developed system of agriculture without any apparent compelling necessity, or any preliminary stages. It seems to have started at the highest level right from the beginning.

The Negev plateau has some peculiar climatic conditions compared to other desert areas on the earth. The adjoining dry areas on the Sinai peninsula and in the Arabian desert only have irregular rainfall.

Figure 32. Horse stables, Shivta.

By contrast, the Negev, which in part rises to nine hundred metres above sea level, can expect regular annual rainfall averaging one hundred millimetres a year, the minimum requirement for agriculture (by comparison, the annual average for London is 600 mm, New York is 1100 mm). However, the rain falls exclusively in the winter months followed by long dry period. The soil is heavy and fertile, but because it is dried out by the heat of the summer, the dense loess soil (see Figure 34) can only absorb and save a small amount of the annual rainfall because the grains of soil expand when wet, thus closing the surface and not allowing the water to soak in. This soil consistency is also the reason for floods which occur in the winter months. If the soil is not worked by human beings, if the surface is not constantly bro-

132

Figure 33. Nabatean dam, collecting fertile soil behind it.

ken up, only a small amount of water seeps into the earth and the rest quickly trains away to the Dead Sea or the Mediterranean in the dry river beds of the wadis which furrow the land (Map 3). Each year there are reports of unsuspecting tourists visiting the Negev in the winter months and putting their lives at risk because of flash floods. More people drown in the desert than die of thirst.

Next to the fertility of the soil and the climatic conditions, it was above all a revival of ancient Sabean traditions; a profound knowledge of natural processes and hard work which created the conditions for the astonishing revolution which took place in the first century with the development of agriculture. It is most likely that this development started with the cultivation of barley as feed for horses which

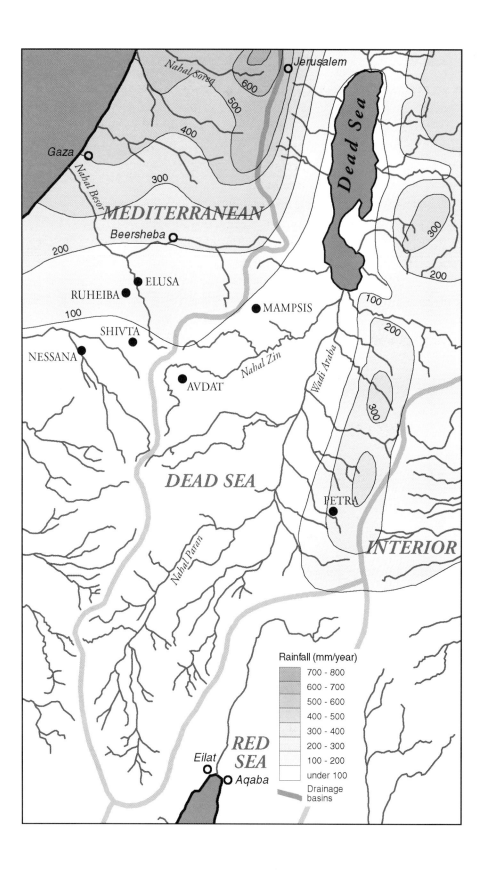

Rainfall (mm/year)

700 - 800
600 - 700
500 - 600
400 - 500
300 - 400
200 - 300
100 - 200
under 100
Drainage basins

were becoming increasingly important. Within a few years the area of land being cultivated for agriculture had expanded to an estimated 3,500 square kilometres.[9] For this an area up to thirty times as large has to be provided with a system of canals in order to provide sufficient irrigation. This meant that more than 100,000 square kilometres was being worked by human hand.

There were many methods to catch and retain the water which flowed as raging torrents on only a few days of the year. Dams were built (Figure 36) and canals were dug which guided the water to the fields. The areas under cultivation were built as terraces so that excess water could flow from the higher to the lower levels (Figure 35). Unfortunately, the irrigation methods used at the time have not yet been thoroughly investigated, as traditional archeology is insufficiently interested in agricultural methods, and agriculturalists have little interest in archeology. That is why specialists often vary greatly in their interpretations.[10]

Agricultural products and methods

Next to pasture land and fields of grain, there were numerous fruit and vegetable gardens, particularly in the surrounding areas of the larger settlements, which provided a large part of the required food. Plantations of fruit trees were established on the edge of the wadis which ran near to the settlements. However, there are many indications that the largest sector of Nabatean agriculture — particularly from the fourth century onwards — consisted of wine growing which clearly developed into one of the most important sources of income for the indigenous population. Vines were cultivated on the broad hillsides running down to the wadis. The stones which cover the desert floor were collected and piled up at regular intervals. The fields, which often extended over an area of several hectares, are still described by the Bedouin as *grape hills* (Figure 38). The piles of stones have a diameter of about one and a half metres, and are approximately eighty centimetres high. Academics are still not certain about their exact function. They agree only that they were probably used for the cultivation of vines. The only place where similar formations have

Map 3. Rainfall and river drainage of the Negev.   135

Figure 35. Nabatean irrigation system near Shivta. It was repaired and trees were planted by M Evenari in the 1950s. The trees still bear fruit today being watered exclusively by the Nabatean system of canals.

< Figure 34. Cracks in the loess soil occurring during the dry season in the Negev.

Figure 36. Nabatean dam near Mampsis.

Figure 37. Partly reconstructed wine press, Avdat. Similar complexes can be found also in other Negev cities.

been found is Wadi Hadramaut at the edge of ancient Saba,[11] another indication to possible origins of Negev agriculture.

Despite the highly developed technology which made agriculture possible in the desert, we must not overlook that it was the constant labour of working the soil which produced such results. Extensive areas were used as catchment areas for rainwater. The construction and maintenance of irrigation equipment made a strict social order necessary. Enormous amounts of soil had to be moved before a functioning irrigation system could be completed, and the maintenance of dams, canals, reservoirs and cisterns could not be done by private initiatives alone. We can see from the papyrus scrolls of Nessana that there was a list of inhabitants of Shivta who took it in turns to clean the city's water reservoirs. The whole population of the city was jointly responsible for preserving this vital part of its existence.

Wine growing as a primary source of income

We know from historical records that the development of agriculture in the Negev coincided with the spread of Christianity. It began shortly after the birth of Christ and reached its high point in the fourth and fifth centuries, before declining and coming to end in the eighth century. The transition from a nomadic existence and trading in incense and myrrh to a settled lifestyle and the cultivation of wine and other agricultural products, as well as the adoption of Christianity represent radical but peaceful incisions in Nabatean cultural development. Over a period of a thousand years, the Nabateans and tribes which joined them traded and grew products which were of paramount importance for religious ceremonies: incense, myrrh and, finally, wine which had already played a role in the original blessing in Jerusalem celebrated by Abraham and Melchizedek (Gen.14:18).

The remains of huge wine presses have been found in Avdat, Elusa and Shivta (Figure 37). They must have been used jointly by a large number of wine growers. In Shivta alone there were three large presses of this kind. The cultivation of wine must have assumed a scale which justified the construction of communal presses. Other agricultural equipment, such as oil mills, lagged far behind in size. During the summer grape picking period, it was possible to press several tonnes of grapes in Shivta alone. The wine from Elusa had an excellent reputation and was repeatedly praised in the writings of the Byzantine age.

The end of Nabatean civilization

The Islamic invasion of 638 triggered a wave of emigration which finally led to the end of Nabatean civilization. Ever larger numbers of people left the Negev. In time, Christianity was no longer tolerated, taxes had risen so high that it was no longer worthwhile to continue with agricultural production. In less than a hundred and fifty years population numbers had been reduced to such an extent that the desert had reasserted itself in the face of a civilization which had lasted for seven hundred years. Only stone remains showed evidence of its

Figure 38. Aerial photograph of the so-called vine hills (Tuleilat al-Anab) near Shivta.

former existence. For centuries, the ruins of Nabatean settlements remained untouched, were neither built on nor vandalized, and were thus left to modern research in a comparatively good state of preservation. Only a few people remained in the region and returned to the same nomadic lifestyle as that of their ancestors when they entered the Negev more than a thousand years ago. No one cared any longer about the existing buildings and agricultural sites which were abandoned and allowed to fall into disrepair. A few traditions from the Nabatean age have been preserved in the customs and habits of the Bedouin today. They have preserved many names from those ancient times, and their knowledge made it much easier to decipher the riddles which faced academics when they started to investigate the unique phenomena of Nabatean culture.

Figure 39. Bedouin woman making butter, Petra.

CHAPTER SIX

Nabateans and Judeans — Contrasting Neighbours

Hitherto, the Hebrew-Judean and Nabatean peoples have been compared mainly on an economic or political level. Without wishing to neglect these aspects, we will attempt here to look specifically at their lifestyle and attitudes as a people. It is not only their geographical proximity which suggests such a comparison. Significant characteristics of the one culture often appear in the other in the opposite form and this alone provides reason enough to compare them. What was of interest to the one would be avoided by the other, what the one assimilated as outside influences was rejected by the other. As well as looking at the purely historical facts we will therefore also attempt to throw some light on the characteristics of the Nabateans by contrasting them with their Judean counterpart.

Writings and traditions

As we have already mentioned, we know of very few Nabatean written documents apart from the numerous inscriptions. Hope lives on among researchers that there are Nabatean documents which still await discovery, as happened with the Dead Sea scrolls found near Qumran, or with the gnostic library of Nag Hammadi which came to light in the 1940s. The sixth-century scholar, Stephen of Byzantium, based his work about the nations, *Ethnica,* on lost writings which could contain valuable information about the Nabateans.[1] The fact that such documents are missing has often led to the assumption that they never existed, but although Stephen's reference is the only one to contemporary Nabatean history, there are numerous indications suggesting that it was common among the Nabateans as well, to make at least a limited written record of some historical events. The Nabateans developed their own script which can be considered to be the original form of present-day Arabic writing, and it is hardly credible that such a highly developed civilization did not produce its own literature.

The use of writing appears to have been widespread among the Nabatean population — something which was uncommon in classical antiquity. Research indicates that at the time of Christ less than ten per cent of the people in Judea could write. Against this background, the extremely mundane content of some Nabatean inscriptions and graffiti which occur in great numbers on the walls of rock in Wadi Haggag on the Sinai peninsula, but also in other places, stand out. Often it was the name of a caravan trader or pilgrim which was scratched into the stone.[2] This means that even people who did not belong to a scholarly or religious cast could write; at least to the extent that they could reproduce their own name. This makes it all the more necessary to ask to what extent the Nabateans also had an oral tradition by which mythical, religious and historical content was passed on, as is common today among the Bedouin in the desert. As we know, many an oral national epic was written down by chance, mostly by outsiders, and was thus preserved from being completely forgotten.[3] The Nabatean world of the gods was so diverse that it was very likely reflected in many stories and traditions. In addition, many merchants lived among the Nabateans who were constantly on their travels. In all civilizations, such people were — and still are — the source of many mythical and historical tales.

The Judean people possessed an immense wealth of writings which originated specifically at the time when Nabatean civilization also reached its climax. Originally, the mythology of the Jews was also passed down orally and formed a comprehensive body of narrative during the last pre-Christian centuries. It was written down in the second and sixth centuries and has been preserved in this codified form up to the present day. The Talmud, with its two main parts, the *Mishnah* and the *Gemara,* contains a large number of such texts. They provide a completely different idea of God from the one found among the Nabateans (for details see p. 76). The Nabatean pantheon is inhabited by numerous different divine beings. The ideas of the Nabateans in relation to their divine world were, as in so many other areas, very flexible. Their relationship with the supersensory was subject to constant change. The situation was quite different among the Judeans: the one and only God who told Abraham to leave Ur in Chaldea for the Promised Land (around 1800 BC) and who continued to live in the consciousness of his descendants, has remained the same into the present. The Judean image of God has shown itself to be immutable and has resisted the change of time.

In the years around the time of the birth of Christ, all the Judean lands, with the exception of the Mediterranean coastal areas bordered the Nabatean kingdom. The earliest mentions of the Nabateans already indicate that they were Arabs.[4] It can therefore be assumed with considerable certainty that all references to *Arabic* in Jewish sources between the fourth century BC and the second century AD, are synonymous with *Nabatean.* For although there were Arabs of different origins, they had little contact with Judea. Egypt, which played an important role for the Jews, was not at that time considered to be part of the Arab world. (Only with the spread of Islam was Egypt included in the Arabic world.) The lack of authentic Nabatean sources means that much of our knowledge about Nabatean history comes from Jewish accounts. Here it is not only their content, reflecting the historical events, which is of importance. The particular way in which their Arabic neighbours were described, judged and, indeed, ignored by the Jewish side shows the sentiments which were extended towards the Nabateans. The unusual quantity of writings which are still in existence provide a noticeable contrast to the almost total lack of Nabatean sources.

One important document in which Jewish civilization at the time of Christ was described from a largely objective point of view is Josephus' *Contra Apion.* Josephus came from a Jewish priestly family. He was brought up to be a priest and, according to his own account, spent a part of his youth with a hermit in the desert. He subsequently turned freedom fighter, leading the revolt against the Romans in Galilee, and was a contemporary of Jesus. After a fateful meeting with Aspasian, a Roman general, he changed over to the Romans and became the historian of one of the most interesting periods in the history of the Jewish people. The description which follows below, illustrates some characteristics of the Jews:

> Here, then, are we, the Jews: we live neither on the coast nor does trading fill our hearts with joy. And that is why we do not visit foreign peoples for our cities are far distant from the sea. Our land is good and fertile and we cultivate its soil. And the highest thing for us is to educate our sons in the spirit of the Torah [the five Books of Moses] and the commandments. The purpose of our life is to maintain these laws and the Torah, our veneration of God, which is transmitted therein. In addition, it is our particular lifestyle which preserved us from mixing with the Greeks among us ...[5]

By contrast, the Nabatean outlook might be paraphrased thus:

> *Here, then, are we, the Nabateans: our kingdom reaches to the coast. Trade fills our hearts with joy. We constantly visit foreign peoples. Some of our cities lie on the coast. Our land is desolate and infertile yet we cultivate its soil. We have no written laws, we venerate many gods and are open to Greek civilization without thereby abandoning our own identity.*

We have already illustrated that Nabatean civilization was astonishingly diverse and flexible, and knew, on the one hand, how to preserve its typical characteristics while, on the other hand, passing through mighty transformations without losing its independence. Like the Jews, the Nabateans also developed a script of their own.[6] It can still be seen today in hundreds of inscriptions on durable material like stone or clay and was used in the Nabatean region into the fourth and fifth centuries AD, in addition to a number of other scripts.[7] There is therefore no basis to the claim that the Nabateans were an illiterate people. The Judeans, in turn, were the exception in classical antiquity because of their comprehensive literature. They demonstrate a completely different attitude to the preservation and passing down of texts. It appears that Judean culture was carried by a relatively small group of literate people. These so-called *scribes* were the spiritual leaders of their people and also ensured that the cultural heritage of their fathers were preserved.

A large part of the Nabatean population travelled frequently, being caravan merchants. These people could maintain contact with their families and households only by the written exchange of news. The maintenance of trade relations with foreign peoples also made it essential that large sections of the population could read and write. Yet this widespread literacy did not, by all appearances, lead to the systematic compilation of Nabatean history, as happened in the case of their northern neighbours in Judea. The spiritual leaders of the Nabateans do not appear to have placed particular value on written records of their laws and customs, although life in the desert would not have been possible without a strictly regulated order.

Settled roots and nomadic rootlessness

In order to illuminate the fundamental differences between both civilizations, we will pick a few further aspects from the numerous points of comparison between the neighbouring peoples of Judea and Nabatea. From a geographical perspective, both kingdoms can be considered as a single territorial unit. The one was a definite desert culture, while for the other, life in the desert represented a myth from a period which, although it was a significant one, was brief and far in the past: the forty years of the Exodus from Egypt. The Judeans were primarily a mountain people tied to the soil. For them, God's promise which had taken them to their land was sacred (compare Gen.13:14). They considered their land to be the setting where God had descended to earth, and a place of revelation. The Temple in Jerusalem formed the focus of the divine presence on earth. The Nabateans, in contrast, were a nomadic people and even in later periods when they had set-

tled down they retained characteristics of their former nomadic existence, never establishing comparably close links with the locality
where they lived. Territorial attachment was not a Nabatean characteristic and never became part of their way of thinking. Neither was
the presence of God tied to a specific spot for them. On the contrary,
it was an inner experience irrespective of where one happened to be.
The Nabateans never had a Holy Land.

Of the twelve tribes of Israel, the descendants of the twelve sons
of Jacob, only two returned from Babylonian captivity in 445 BC: the
tribe of Levi, which produced the priests of the temple, and the tribe
of Judah, which gave the Jewish people and their land their name. The
appropriate designation for all twelve tribes is Hebrews (Ivri), which
means (all names have a meaning in Hebrew) 'those who travel by,
the travellers.'

Although the Hebrews were not a nomadic people, they were
forced to wander from one place to another during their long history.
As we have already mentioned in connection with Nabatean history,
the name *Nabatean* also had its characteristic meaning and was connected with the concept of *sprouting, germinating:* terms which do
not indicate a nomadic people and which are connected, paradoxically, with existence tied to a specific place. But what is it that comes
to expression in the names of these peoples?

In both cases, the Nabateans and the Judeans were originally tribal
groups which had emerged from larger ethnic groups. Both peoples
— and this they have in common — were immigrants who came from
faraway to the country where their civilization later flourished. Thus
Jewish civilization arose on leaving Mesopotamia which lies north of
the land promised to them; Nabatean civilization developed in extremely fertile territory south of the region where they would later
settle, the country of Saba (compare p. 63). Yahweh promised the
descendants of Jacob, the grandson of Abraham, the common ancestor of both peoples, a land 'flowing with milk and honey' (Exod.3:8).
However, the angel who foretold the birth of Ishmael, the tribal ancestor of the Nabateans, to his mother, Hagar, prophesied a 'wild' future for him (Gen.16:11f). Both prophecies were to come true in the
destiny of the two peoples.

Monotheism, the belief in a single God, appears for the first time in human history in the ancient Hebrew people as a national religion. The exclusive and direct nature with which God the creator lives in the consciousness of the people, and the direct dialogue between God and human beings which is thus enabled, creates a more intimate relationship between the creator and his creation. The expectation of the Messiah, who was to be physically revealed, produced within Hebrew civilization a special need for a God-willed ordering of life in this world. God's representative would only appear in a community of people who adhered to God-given morality, codes and laws. That is why precise regulations and instructions were observed in dealing with the world created by God in order to ensure purity; even the soil was too old in accordance with divine guidance. Thus the Hebrews paradoxically became people who directed their attention towards material existence in expectation of the divine revelation.

The Nabateans were surrounded by an external world in which there were few traces of life. They experienced the mineral world as lifeless formations which did not respond to their questioning look, but guided them to perceive the existence of the supersensible. The consciousness of the Nabateans was directed towards a realm which was the source of life in human beings and nature, an existential plane on which the life forces exist and to which their senses had been awakened. The knowledge of how to bring a highly developed civilization into existence in the desert, how to turn the scorching sun into a life-giving force, the effective use of the all too scarce resource of water — all of this indicates that it was not fixed moral laws and rules which dominated the encounter with the physical world here. In antiquity, there was a clear awareness of the connection between human beings and the four elements of nature, earth, air, fire and water. The element of water was understood as the material expression of the formative or etheric forces which are active in all living things. The Nabateans had a particularly intimate relationship not with the mineral world, but with this realm of life, and the forces which were able to transform the hostile desert into a fertile landscape. This comes to expression, too, in their name: *Nabateans,* which means in a general sense someone 'who deals with things that sprout and germinate.'

Solomon and the Queen of Sheba

From all that we know about the origins of the Nabateans, we can consider them to be the descendants of Sabean tribes which left their southern Arabian homeland and emigrated to the Negev. The quintessential meeting between the Nabateans and the Hebrews is reported in the Old Testament (1Kings 10:1–13) as the visit of the Queen of Sheba to King Solomon.

> Now when the queen of Sheba heard of the fame of Solomon concerning the name of the Lord, she came to test him with hard questions.

It must have been a mysterious encounter at which Solomon was confronted with questions and which continues to pose even more riddles for posterity which have been linked to this 'summit meeting.'

The description in the book of Kings is exceedingly short. There are only a few coded clues in the brief description which show something of the significance of this event. For King Solomon, this meeting represented a kind of biographical turning point. From this point onwards the Bible only reports his decadence. He falls prey to his worldly interests, increases the size of his harem, prays to idols, and turns away from his faith in Yahweh. The late Jewish tradition sees the Queen of Sheba as the force which triggered this marked turning point in the life of Solomon. Her heathen influence is said to have been so dominant that Solomon was deflected from his original cast of mind, and is why the Queen of Sheba was regarded as a demonic figure in Jewish culture up into the late Middle Ages. The Babylonian King Nebuchadnezzar, whose army destroyed Jerusalem and the first Temple of Solomon in the sixth century BC, is depicted in legend as the descendant of the Queen of Sheba and Solomon.[8] Here we find one of the reasons for the ambiguous relationship between the Judeans and the Nabateans which dominated the history of both peoples. It is influenced on the Jewish side, on the one hand, by a recognition of the high level of spirituality of Nabatean culture; the

Nabateans are respected neighbours. On the other hand an attempt is made to counter Nabatean thought. They are thus mentioned in documents mostly as *Arabs* and are referred to as little as possible.

Religious ceremonies and sacrifice

The direct distance between Petra and Jerusalem is only about 150 kilometres. Both the Nabateans and the Judeans founded their capitals in the mountains. In both cases they were simultaneously political and religious centres. The same applied to the pilgrimage sites where the people made sacrifices at specific times. Animals were sacrificed both in Jerusalem and in Petra up to the time of the destruction of the second Jewish temple in AD 70. In Jerusalem, this ceremony took place in the Temple. The Holy of Holies in the inner part of the temple remained hidden to the public and the sacrifice itself took place only in the presence of the priests. The opposite applied to the Nabateans: animal sacrifices were carried out further away from the people, not in an enclosed space but on the high mountain tops in the open air so that the fire and smoke could be seen from the valley. Such places of sacrifice can still be seen in Petra (see Figure 8). It was not until shortly before the birth of Christ, during the last pre-Christian century when the sacrifice of animals ceased, that the Nabateans began to build temples made of stone. They too were concerned with death but no longer with the violent sacrifice of animals but with tracing the path of the human soul on its way into the heavenly realms after death. Nabatean religious ceremonies were not dependent on the locality where they took place. In the case of Petra, the site of the capital was chosen above all for strategic reasons. While Jerusalem offers some advantages for its defence, the location of the city was chosen for its religious significance.[9] However, whereas Petra with its overwhelming monuments lost its importance as a spiritual and political centre with the rise of Christianity and the loss of the state sovereignty of the Nabatean kingdom, Jerusalem has retained its central importance for three world religions, Judaism, Christianity and Islam, to the present day.

Remembrance and forgetting

Remembrance and forgetting are another aspect we can compare. Jews and Nabateans related to the old traditions in quite different ways. In Jewish culture the preservation of the past has become a sacred duty and has developed into one of the dominant features of the Jewish character, determining political and religious actions in all ages. The Judeans considered the word of God, which had proclaimed the law to them, as sacred. The laws were preserved and respected — and they apply to the present day.

The ancient Hebrews became a people during the four hundred years in Egyptian slavery. 'But the descendants of Israel were fruitful and increased greatly, they multiplied, and grew exceedingly strong; so that the land was filled with them.' (Exod.1:7) Here there is a similarity with the Nabateans, of whom there were only about ten thousand in the Negev desert and east of Wadi Araba in the fourth century BC, according to Diodorus' description.[10] Both peoples had their origins far from their later homeland and were characterized by rapid population growth.

The changeable history of the ancient Hebrew people began with the Exodus from Egypt, and was permeated with the constant reminder of the past and their significance as the chosen people. They constantly had to be newly reminded by the prophets, of the divine promise and the expectations expressed by Yahweh in his revelation on Mount Sinai. The people always displayed a tendency to turn away from monotheism. They created a golden calf and worshipped it, even while Moses was receiving the divine revelation on the mountain, (Exod.32). Jewish history can be understood as a constant struggle to preserve the word of God which was once heard by the Jewish people. It shows a continuous tendency to reject foreign influences and focus on its own roots and origins.

The Nabateans understood something quite different by maintaining their tradition. For them it did not mean keeping centuries of tradition unchanged and passing it on to their descendants. Traditional things were always seen as the starting point for new developments. It was a civilization of openness and transformation. What the guardians of Nabatean civilization thought worth preserving was something which was in a constant state of renewal.

Isolation and interchange

Researchers the world over prefer to study those peoples who are linked to their own origins and traditions. In Israel there is intensive research into Judaism, in Europe interest is primarily directed at the roots of Christianity when looking at the history of the Holy Land. Other groups of peoples, of which there are many in Palestine, are neglected, starting with the seven nations which Joshua had to overcome after the Exodus from Egypt[11] and extending to the Samaritans and former soldiers of the Byzantine army. Thus the Nabateans were neglected by academics for a long time as well, perhaps also because they resist clear ethnic classification and thus present many historians with difficulties. However, it is this characteristic in particular which should arouse our interest.

The cosmic mission of the Jewish people was to prepare the conditions for the physical body of Jesus. Thus the path of a person who wanted to convert to the Jewish religion was made very difficult. For the rest of their life they was stuck with the label *stranger*. According to the law of Moses, he possessed the same rights but was not really equal to someone who was Judean by origin.[12] On the other hand they were treated with greater leniency regarding the strict fulfilment of their religious duties. These efforts at ethnic separation must not be understood as the dubious striving to preserve the purity of one's own *race*. We are dealing here with a principle which was repeatedly and always broken when it was a matter of introducing new spiritual impulses into Judaism. Then *foreign blood* was mixed with the Hebrew. Thus Moses had a Midianite wife and Ruth, David's ancestor, was a Moabite (Ruth 4:22).

The actions of the Nabateans once again contrast completely with this. They attempted to isolate themselves neither on an ethnic nor on a religious level and multiplied not only when they were away from their homeland but also mixed with the local indigenous population, as happened when they settled in the Negev. The mass immigration after the Islamic invasion allows us to assume that no great value was placed on the preservation of an ethnic identity.

The Sabeo-Nabatean migration into the Negev is likely to have started with a relatively small tribal group. The Nabateans, too, were originally an ethnically homogenous group from the same people or tribe, and were bound to the same spiritual stream. Diodorus estimates their number at ten thousand but this is likely to have grown considerably over the following millennium. In the Negev alone the population grew three or fourfold up to the time of Christ, and at least as many people again lived in the remaining provinces of the Nabatean kingdom.[13] This rapid growth in population is a unique phenomenon in the classical world, but such population growth can also be explained by other tribes joining the original immigrants and adapting to their way of life. Anyone who felt Nabatean could call himself such irrespective of his origins. The prosperity of the region was undoubtedly a factor which promoted immigration, but the reasons for the integration and assimilation of immigrants cannot be explained by this reason alone. On the contrary, wealth and the reluctance to share it would have been an argument against accepting strangers as equal citizens.

After the end of the Nabatean kingdom, the traces of the former immigrants became so obscured both in ethnic and cultural terms that some researchers are inclined no longer to call them Nabateans but *Byzantines*,[14] using archeological finds from this period to support their argument. It is evident, however, that the stylistic elements found in Shivta are quite distinct from finds in the north of the country as well as in the whole of the Byzantine area.[15] Avraham Negev takes the opposite view and considers the inhabitants of the Negev to be the direct descendants of those tribes which are thought to have migrated to the area in the sixth century BC,[16] making reference to inscriptions with Nabatean names[17] which were used from the beginning of the Nabatean presence in the Negev. Although this could be interpreted as indicating a certain continuity in the Nabatean tradition, and also, therefore, of ethnic consciousness, many Greek, Roman, Hebrew and other names also appear. Nevertheless, it is precisely this connection between new and old, between what is foreign and what is most essentially their own which appears to give these people the right to call themselves Nabatean. The question as to the identity of these *late Nabateans* in the Byzantine period can therefore not be answered using ethnicity as a basis.

Restriction and openness

The wish for exclusiveness, which was completely alien to the Nabateans, is not only evident in the Jewish people in terms of their ethnicity. Judea was always surrounded by clear state boundaries. The Mediterranean formed the clear western border. The imaginary line from Gaza to the Gulf of Aqaba separated the kingdom from the Sinai peninsula during its greatest territorial expansion at the time of King Solomon (approximately 800 BC). The River Jordan formed the eastern frontier. After the return from Babylonian exile in 445 BC, Judea extended no further than the southern tip of the Dead Sea and ended at that natural frontier which divides the agricultural land from the desert region to the south. What applied to the state territory as a whole also applied to its cities, which although they occupied strategically favourable positions on the mountain heights, were also surrounded by strong walls, which few Nabatean settlements had.

Nabatean rule extended over a less clearly defined territory. A clear frontier was only apparent where the kingdom bordered Judea. A glance at the map shows that the exact drawing of borders in the extensive and sparsely populated area inhabited by the Nabateans would not have meant a great deal in any case. Although there were no natural borders in the south and the east, it was there that the trade routes ran which radiated out into neighbouring regions, reaching as far as distant India (see Map 5).[18] They served not only the trade in goods but were also the means of lively cultural interchange between the different peoples. The Nabatean sphere of influence thus extended to the farthest regions. In return, the influence of foreign civilizations penetrated deep into the core of Nabatean territory.

War and peace

Although the Judeans were known in the classical world for their high degree of spirituality and closeness to God, they always had to assert or defend their spiritual and material interests by use of military power. This was connected not least with the geographical position of their country which then, as now, formed an important interface between East and West. It was the fate of any people settling there never to be allowed to rest its arms. Whether this was owing to the eagerness to enter the fray or because of necessity, in either case the constant readiness for battle informed the thinking of a population in which the sword was passed on from generation to generation to defend their Holy Land.

Different circumstances prevailed in the Nabatean kingdom. This country, too, formed a bridge between East and West, but only the Nabateans understood how to cross this bridge owing to their familiarity with desert conditions. A journey from the Mediterranean to southern Arabia or India was possible only by joining a Nabatean caravan. The Nabateans moved through the desert like a ferryman across a river. The latter never leaves the water but without him no one can cross the river. The Nabateans were clever traders and merchants who had achieved wealth and prosperity, but they were no warriors. Their army served only to protect the caravan stations from robbers. It defended their interests, not their territory. The Nabateans formed a civilization which had only a dim sense of its mission in world history, but which did not seek to achieve its aims by physical force.

The history of the Nabateans, to the extent that it can be continuously traced, shows that the military conflicts in which they were involved were either of a defensive nature or served to re-establish peace as quickly as possible. The astonishing extent of Nabatean territory was not based on any imperialist ambitions. Diodorus reports Nabatean raids as late as the fourth century BC[19] but he mentions in the same context that these were people with an extreme love of freedom. In the course of this development, during which these shepherd and nomadic tribes coalesced into a kingdom under Hellenistic influence, not only did their love of freedom increase, but also the desire for peace as the essential basis of a free life also grew. Peace was pre-served and cultivated not only externally, but also among the Nabateans themselves. It was a state whose citizens were members of a great diversity of tribes, but in Strabo's words they all 'lived in peace with one another.'[20]

The relationship between both peoples

The history of Judea is a history of wars, victories and defeats. The land promised by God was conquered by force of arms after the Exodus from Egypt and constantly had to be defended. The Old Testament (1Kings, 2Chron.) is full of descriptions of these conflicts which finally resulted in civil war and the division of the kingdom. The Nabateans, by comparison, led a comparatively peaceful life. They avoided armed conflict, and only reacted to force and threats coming from outside. There had to be a special kind of relationship between the Jews and Nabateans to enable the two peoples to live alongside one another largely without conflict, and in respect of each other's particular characteristics.

The earliest mention of political relations between these so very different neighbours occurs, curiously, at the time of the reconsecra-tion of the Temple in Jerusalem in 164 BC, during the Jewish Hasmonean uprising (169–162 BC) against Greek rule. The Nabateans, despite having adopted Greek forms of rulership, were favourably in-clined towards their neighbours' battle against Hellenistic influence, and supported the Judeans in their struggle for independence against the Greeks. Was it a diplomatic tactic or was it respect for another people's need for self-determination and to live in freedom?

Other episodes from the common history of both peoples docu-ment similar behaviour. Following the successful uprising against the Greeks, the Jewish general Judas Maccabeus journeyed through the country with his followers and fought against everything which stood in his way, physically and spiritually. The Hasmonean kingdom which he founded had clearly militaristic traits. His rulership style stood in absolute contrast to the peaceful Nabatean, and yet friendly relations existed between him and Aretas I, the first known Nabatean king. This fundamental attitude did not just emerge after the Jewish struggle for liberation against Greek supremacy. The apocryphal writings of the Maccabees report that Jason, the brother of the High Priest Onias, who purchased his priestly office from the Greek rulers for three hundred silver shillings (2Macc.4:8). After he had been revealed to be corrupt and traitorous he had to flee (2Macc.5:6-10) and sought protection with the Nabatean King, Aretas I, in Petra. However, the latter at first put Jason under arrest and later cast him out, and he died in exile.

Peace was not to exist in Judea under the successors of Judas Maccabeus. Jonathan, his brother, who inherited his power, was murdered by the 'sons of Jambris.' Although they are often described as Nabateans,[21] they are likely to have been a tribe following a different tradition which only came under Nabatean rule as the kingdom spread to the north-east. Accordingly, the Book of Maccabees also distinguishes between them and the Nabateans:

> He [Jonathan] sent his brother Johanan at the head of his troops to the *Nabateans who loved him* to ask them whether they would look after all his baggage. But the sons of Jambris from Medeba went out, took Johanan with all he had with him and took him with them. (1Macc.9:35f)

The friendly feelings towards the neighbouring Judeans will have been based not least on their common religious convictions. Although Nabatean civilization was influenced by Hellenism to a greater extent, it shared the Jewish ban on images and refrained from depicting God in art. The sculptures on the Petran monuments which were created shortly before the time of Christ were defaced to the extent that human faces can no longer be recognized (see p. 107).

The influence of Hellenism

There are periods in the history of both peoples when a turn to Hellenism predominated. Various inscriptions and coins even show that Aretas III was given the epithet *Philhellenos* — 'he who loves

Greek civilization.'[22] Yet this pro-Hellenic tendency came to expression in completely different ways in the Judeans and Nabateans. Whereas the former modelled themselves on the Greek armies in their conquests and acts of war, the Nabateans profited above all, from Greek culture, on a religious, spiritual and artistic level.

Although one might think that in addition to the numerous contrasts between Judeans and Nabateans their different relationships with Greek culture might have led to possible tensions between the two peoples, the opposite happened, as history illustrates. This can be seen not only in the behaviour of Aretas I and his support for the rebels in Judea, but also in the reverse in that at times, when both turned to Greek civilization, their relationship simultaneously deteriorated. At such times it was no longer cultural exchange and mutual fertilization in the spiritual field which stood in the foreground, but personal quests for power and purely economic interests.

At the turn of the second to the first century BC, a Hellenophile, power-hungry ruler, Alexander Jannaeus, came to power in Judea who crowned himself king. He snatched part of the Nabatean territory east of the Jordan and the port of Gaza, which was vital to their trade, since the majority of the goods brought by Nabatean caravans from the Far East was shipped to Egypt from there. The temporary loss of the port cast a shadow over relations between the two peoples for a while. King Aretas III, who ascended the throne in 87 BC, reconquered the coast; but he refrained from further military campaigns and despite having defeated Alexander Jannaeus, made peace with him and withdrew from the country. Josephus describes these events in the following words:

> After these events, the people of Damascus brought Aretas, the Arab, into their country out of hatred for Ptolemy [the ruler of Egypt] and made him king over the Syrian armies. He attacked Judea, beat Alexander Jannaeus in war, but concluded a peace alliance with him and left the country.[23]

Josephus' remarks show clearly how Damascus came under Nabatean rule. Aretas III was called upon by the population to take over as ruler in a difficult situation. This happened about 60 BC. The Nabatean assumption of power was neither the result of a thirst for power not did it serve economic interests. Even if this act of help might seem insignificant in itself, the voluntary withdrawal must be seen as an event the like of which has rarely happened in world history. Against this background, the voluntary renunciation of state sovereignty in 106 AD and subjugation to Roman sovereignty appears as a much more credible move.

Conflict or competition

According to Strabo's reports, the Nabatean king shared his office with the *Epitropos,* a chancellor with far-reaching powers: 'The city is ruled by a man from the royal house and the king has one of his friends, who is called his 'brother,' as governor.'[24] The king himself was concerned with religious, cultural and cultic affairs (see p. 56). As the priest king, he was the real spiritual leader of his people. More worldly affairs were the responsibility of the *Epitropos.* The fate of one of these *Epitropoi,* Syllaeus, takes a particular place Nabatean history. He ruled at the side of Obodas III (30–9 BC) and assumed a dominant position. When Aretas IV succeeded the deceased king, he was not yet of age; Syllaeus was scheming, hungry for power and false, and ruthlessly used the inexperience of the new king for his own ends. In doing so, he involved the kingdom in many senseless battles. Several conflicts took place in the border areas of Nabatea and Judea, which was ruled by Herod the Great, in a short period of tension between the two states, since the rulers on both sides were pursuing expansionist aims. In the final years of his life, Syllaeus supported acts of terrorism against Judea in southern Syria. In 6 BC he was condemned to death in Rome and executed on the orders of Emperor Augustus.[25]

In Judea, the power of the king was fundamentally restricted to worldly affairs. Service in the Temple, the ritual and the religious leadership of the people lay in the hands of the priestly caste. Their clerical tasks included ensuring that the leaders of the state respected the laws given by God. It was only in times of decline that the Judean rulers also appropriated the office of High Priest.

In the period of armed conflict between Nabatea and Judea the usual mode of government, with its various divisions of power, had been disturbed on both sides. On the one side, there was Syllaeus who had exceeded his responsibilities in order to satisfy his thirst for power, and was thus working counter to the traditions of his people. On the other side, there was Herod who, just as hungry for power, threatened to appropriate the priestly role. The Judean lands had become a vassal state of the Roman Empire. It was only the presence of the Roman army which secured Herod's power. The previously highly developed religious life with the first monotheistic religion in human history, now sank to an unprecedented level of decadence. Herod was half Edomite. He was popularly described as an *Edomite slave.* In terms of his descent, he was closer to the Nabateans than to the Jews. So it is not surprising that a non-Jew, who only ruled by the grace of the Romans, who was hated by the people, and who interfered crudely in the mysteries and rituals of the Temple, should also be prepared to accept the deterioration in relations, otherwise so harmonious, with his Nabatean neighbours.

If at other times state and, above all, cultural relations between the two peoples were conducted harmoniously, this harmony was considerably upset during the time of Herod. Their different views and habits, and the contrasts in their understanding of the world, had enabled interchange between them to be free of competition. They were moving alongside one another not against one another. However, this exceptional situation created a convergence in the political objectives of both states in which similar interests clashed. As soon as the otherwise contrasting tendencies of the two neighbours appeared to converge, bloody conflict arose.

Different forms of rule

Whereas Greek civilization had clearly influenced the way of doing things at the Nabatean court, in Judea the same traditional forms of rule were maintained as before the destruction of the first Temple in 586 BC.

160

The second Book of Kings reports on the events which occurred at the courts of the divided kingdom after Solomon's rule, which ended with the destruction of the first Temple. The religious behaviour of the Judean and Israelite kings would be worthy of a book in itself, as they oscillated ceaselessly between belief in the one God who had revealed himself to Moses on Mount Sinai, and the polytheistic cults of the neighbouring pagans. A direct link is made by the author of the Old Testament text between the duration of a king's rule, the success of his political objectives and his faith. If the king served Yahweh, he was blessed with success and long life. If, however, he fell prey to idolatry he only deserved a short rule.[26] Curiously, the first king of the split-off kingdom of Israel, whose cult of the dead and fire burials are reported with disdain by the biblical authors, was called Jeroboam son of Nebat. The root consonants of his name, N-B-T, found in the word Nabatean, seem to indicate an alien influence which was anathema to Judaic religion.

The period when the Nabatean kings ruled was a relatively short one. It lasted from the second century BC to AD 106. If the Judean king clearly exceeded his responsibilities when he intervened in religious affairs, priestly functions formed the actual task of the Nabatean kings, some of whom ruled for more than thirty years. They were always more deeply involved in the religious life than in the administration of the kingdom.

The way in which the people venerate the king was also different in character. The Judean rulers had all too human traits according to the biblical account. None of them were considered to be infallible, none of them were elevated to divine status, as happened with the later Roman emperors, and worshipped as such. With the Nabateans, the king was under scrutiny from his subjects. Strabo reports: 'Often he [the king] justified himself to his people; and on occasion even his lifestyle came under scrutiny.'[27]

Perhaps it was precisely this requirement to provide an account of his actions which not only secured the popularity of the king, but also ensured that Obodas was elevated to divine status in accordance with Roman custom. Today we can still see the remains of a temple dedicated to him in Avdat, the city which carries his name (Figure 40).[28]

Figure 40. Entrance to the temple of Obodas, third century AD, Avdat.

Christianity and religious awareness

The nearer the time came to when Jesus would be born, the more strongly the approach and development of new spiritual and religious impulses was perceived in the spiritual centres of the classical world. Such an awareness was developed particularly strongly within Judaism. The scrolls which have been found at the Dead Sea near to the border between Judea and Nabatea indicate that the Essenes already had a precise concept half-century before the birth of Jesus, of an original sacrament as represented in the Christian Eucharist. The thought of a divine being taking on human form occupied the whole of the known world at that time.[29] Rudolf Steiner notes that an idea of the coming of this event was taking shape in various different civilizations at this time. The birth of Jesus not only introduced a new calendar, it also marked a short moment in the history of the world when various spiritual streams came together in a common spiritual understanding and in comparable spiritual endeavours, to create the basis on which Christianity could develop into a world religion.

The contrast between Judea and Nabatea can also be looked at in the context of the different contributions with which both peoples influenced the development of Christianity. The silencing of the divine voice was experienced in a tragic fashion within Judaism. As a result, an analytical attitude became dominant in its spiritual and religious life. The only source of knowledge was the tradition in which the divine word was captured. In order to understand the will of God, the religious writings through which he spoke had to be studied and interpreted. This meant that the writings which were handed down had to be kept as pure as possible, protected from falsifying influences and kept away foreign thought which did not come directly from Judaism's own sources. If the divine revelation had originally been intended for all the people, it was now preserved within a small circle of scribes. There is a place in the Talmud from the time of Christ which clearly sets out this attitude: 'Moses received the Torah on Sinai and handed it to Joshua; Joshua to the elders, the elders to the prophets, and the prophets gave it to the men of the great synagogue. They spoke three words: be mild in judgement, take many pupils, and build a fence around the teaching.'[30]

This 'fence' had to be erected because the divine revelation had grown silent and the things which could be gathered from this source of wisdom had to be preserved for future generations. Everything which might endanger these extremely valuable goods was meant to stay outside the fence.

The birth of Jesus and the creation of Christianity also represented a turning point in the destiny of the people of these two fundamentally different neighbours. Judaism prepared Christianity on a material and genetic level. Jesus was born into the Jewish people, lived almost the whole of his life in Palestine and was crucified in Jerusalem in direct proximity to the temple. A few years later in the year 70, the national uprising of the Jews was bloodily put down by the Romans and the Temple was razed to the ground. From this time on Jews were forbidden to stay in Jerusalem. Three years later, the mass suicide of the inhabitants of Massada on the Dead Sea marked the breaking of the final Jewish resistance as the Judean kingdom ceased to exist.

A few decades later, Nabatea, too, would lose its status as an independent kingdom and become a Roman province, but there events took a completely different course. In 106 AD, the Nabateans of their own free will gave up their independence and subjugated themselves to Roman rule. This smooth and completely peaceful transition meant that little changed in the everyday lives of the population.

The Nabateans experienced the original events in Christianity and Christianization completely differently from the Judeans. Although Christianity had in the meantime spread over the whole of the Mediterranean area, its followers could initially only practise it in secret. During the first three centuries, it was able to develop only in the catacombs, both in a concrete and in a metaphorical sense. One exception was the former Nabatean kingdom. Even under Roman rule, the arm of centralized authority could not reach the inaccessible desert areas of the province now described officially as *Palaestina Salutaris.* No catacombs existed here into which the followers of the new faith had to withdraw. No evidence of the persecution of Christians has ever come to light in this region. For the Nabatean way of thinking the Christian teaching was nothing more than a natural continuation of its own traditions.

The Nabateans rather than the Judeans thus turned out to be the true followers of Christ. They too were living in expectation of the Messiah and they knew of his coming, but they experienced his arrival not on a physical and genetic level but in the sphere of the etheric, life forces with which they were so familiar. As a consequence of centuries of constantly having to deal with the conditions imposed by a harsh desert region, they had developed a sensitivity and special perception for everything which is necessary for life and its preservation.

The Nabateans were the first people in human history — in so far as they can be described as a people — which converted to Christianity en masse. A culture was prevalent among them which on

the basis of its synthetic tendencies could assimilate all things foreign. Despite the renewed flowering of their civilization in Byzantine
times, their existence as a people came to an end shortly after the
Islamic invasion in the seventh century. They left the Negev, and the
environment in which they had lived became barren again. No one has
yet been able to give a clear answer to the question of what happened
to their descendants. Such an action represents a gesture which is similar to their giving up state sovereignty in 106 AD. Both were stages
on the path to the complete renunciation of ethnic identity. The latter
had lost its importance with the transition to Christianity. The gates of
heaven reopened for the Nabateans with the Mystery of Golgotha.
The Christian ritual and its mysteries dissolved all ethnic ties once
and for all.

*Figure 41 (overleaf). Part of the city of Petra, with the Urn Tomb (left) and
Royal Tombs in the background.*

CHAPTER SEVEN

Petra — City of Priests
and Kings

Any depiction of Nabatean civilization would be incomplete without a study of Petra, capital and royal city of Nabatea. Apart from a few inscriptions, there are no written documents which might clearly reveal the secrets of this place.

Up to now, only a small part of the approximately twelve square kilometre city territory has been the subject of archeological excavations. Most of the free-standing buildings have been levelled and there are large areas where there are no buildings at all. Only some of the rock monuments, whose façades were hewn out of the stone, have been exceptionally well preserved. We do not know when the last inhabitants left Petra. It is assumed that it happened during the two centuries following the Islamic invasion of 638. Thereafter, only nomads lived here periodically. Hidden in a rocky valley in the Jordanian mountains with difficult access, the location of the city was soon forgotten and some thousand years had to pass before Johann Ludwig Burckhardt rediscovered it and identified it as the former capital of the Nabateans. Burckhardt's push towards Petra was a risky undertaking. The indigenous Bedouin were concerned to keep the location of the city hidden from strangers for they suspected the existence of significant treasure. Burckhardt could only escape the hostility of the local people by disguising himself as a pilgrim who wished to make a sacrifice on Mount Aaron to fulfil a vow. In the summer of 1812, he reached the city through Wadi Musa. Measured against the magnificent impression which the hitherto unknown buildings must have made on a European visitor, his reports sound exceedingly sober. He was, nevertheless, aware of the extraordinary importance of his discovery:

> Let future travellers visit the place under the protection of an armed troop. The local inhabitants will get used to seeing strangers undertaking research there in their thirst for knowledge, and then people will see that the ancient monuments of Wadi Musa rank among the most interesting of ancient art.[1]

Some hundred and fifty years later, in 1969, P.J. Parr concluded his summary of the first forty years of archeological research in Petra with the words:

> It would be a great mistake to assume that our knowledge today is very detailed or deep. In fact we know very little about the Nabateans and still less about their capital. Petra remains an almost virgin site. It will require another forty years of intensive archeological endeavour before a comprehensive history of Petra can be written.[2]

Quite a few years have passed since that statement without the hope it expresses having been fulfilled. Archeology has still not progressed much further. To the present day it has not been possible to construct a unified and complete picture of the history of the development of Petra and its settlement. Instead of being able to find solutions to problems such as the purpose and meaning of the rock monuments, all research so far has simply thrown up new questions sharpening existing controversies between academics. In view of this lack of tangible and scientifically-based facts, we will not even begin to try and reproduce a comprehensive portrait of Petra. We know too little to be able to reconstruct the fate of this city. Petra continues to remain a riddle. Its solution will have to be left to future generations of researchers. All we can do is to abandon ourselves to the unforgettable impression against which no visitor to this city can be immune.

Figure 42. Block tombs at the entrance to the Siq, Petra.

The legend of the site

The earliest inhabitants of the area around Petra, whose traces still exist, were the Edomites. Many fragments of Edomite pottery from the end of the second millennium BC, were found near Petra. The Nabateans are mentioned for the first time in Diodorus in connection with the campaign by Antigonus Monophthalmos in 312 BC. The same document also refers to a refuge of the Nabateans which is described as *'sela'* that is, *rock*. Although this is often interpreted as Petra, it might have been on the mountain known today as *Umm al-Biyara* (mother of springs) which rises to a height of three hundred and fifty metres above the valley of Petra. Remains of an Edomite settlement were found here and they were known to have settled here in the first millennium BC.

Figure 43 Boulevard with propyleum and temple district, the Dushrat temple (Qasr al-Bint) is in the background.

Towards the east, one can see the whole layout of Petra; towards the West one can look as far as Wadi Araba. The ancestor of the Edomites was Esau, Jacob's brother, who was cheated out of his birthright and the blessing of his father, Isaac (Genesis 27). In Hebrew, the word *edom* means *red* and is also contained in the terms *adam* (human being), *dam* (blood) and *adama* (earth). The Edomites were in fact a people tied to the earth; they lived as warriors and hunters and the Edom mountains have a reddish sheen. They extend south-east from the Dead Sea to the Gulf of Aqaba, and in the southern part reach a height of up to 1600 metres. The name *Petra* means *rock* in Greek and appears for the first time in documents from the Greek period. The meaning of its place name already occurs in the Old Testament in its Hebrew form of *Sela,* such as for example in

Isaiah: 'They have sent the lambs to the ruler of the land from Sela, by way of the desert to the mount of the daughter of Zion.' (Isa.16:1) Petra has been linked with the Nabateans ever since Diodorus' report from the year 312 BC.[3]

Petra lies at the base of a valley surrounded by craggy mountain desert and the winter rains naturally flow through it into Wadi Araba. It forms part of *Wadi Musa* (valley of Moses). The dramatic events which are connected with both the Jewish and the Islamic tradition are described in the Old Testament (Num.20). A mosque was erected on the rock in the village which also bears the name Wadi Musa, and which is situated several kilometres east of Petra. This is said to be the same rock which Moses smote with his rod when the people began to waver in their belief for lack of water:

> And the water came forth abundantly and the congregation drank, and their cattle. And the Lord said to Moses and Aaron: 'Because you did not believe me, to sanctify me in the eyes of the people of Israel, therefore you shall not bring this assembly into the land which I have given them.' (Num.20:11f)

A few kilometres west of Petra we find the *Jabal Harun* — Mount Aaron in English. This is where traditionally Aaron is thought to have been buried. Like Moses, Aaron also died before reaching the land promised by God and could no longer fulfil the sacrifice himself.[4] 'And Aaron the priest went up Mount Hor at the command of the Lord, and died there, in the fortieth year after the people of Israel had come out of the land of Egypt ...' (Num.33:38) According to one legend, the soul of Aaron hovered above Petra looking for its final resting place. The mountains trembled and shattered. Only Mount Hor remained intact.

Petra lies at the site of these legendary events in a landscape wholly composed of rock. Approximately two kilometres distant from the village of Wadi Musa the valley narrows after a sharp bend into a cleft in the rock. This is where the famous *Siq* starts, the gorge which, coming from the east, forms the only entrance into Petra.

Where the cleft in the rock opens, which forms the Siq, it still has

Map 4. Petra.

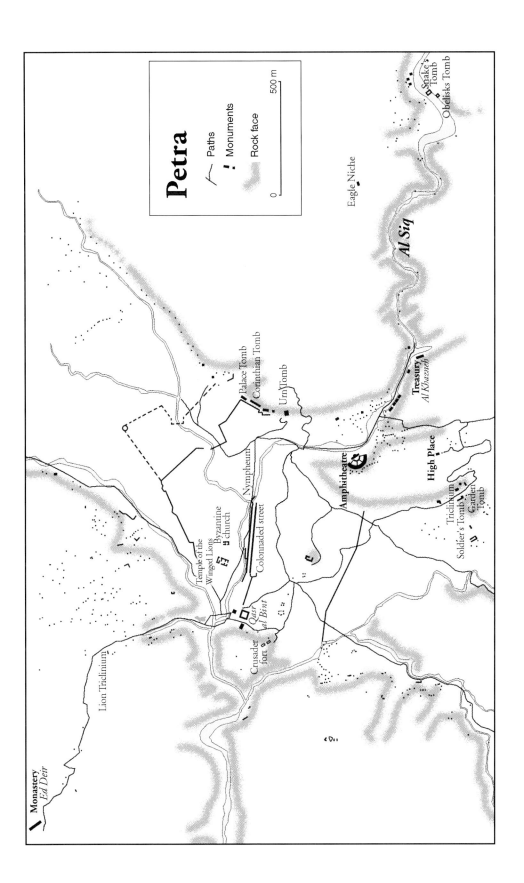

Petra

Paths

Monuments

Rock face

0   500 m

Monastery
Ed Deir

Lion Triclinium

Temple of the
Winged Lions

Byzantine
church

Colonnaded street

Nympheum

*Qasr
al Bint*

Crusader
fort

Palace Tomb

Corinthian Tomb

Urn Tomb

Amphitheatre

High Place

Triclinium

Soldier's Tomb

Garden
Tomb

Eagle Niche

Treasury
Al Khazneh

Al Siq

Snake's
Tomb

Obelisks Tomb

a width of about four to five metres; the walls to the left and the right rise up to fifty metres. The further we progress, the narrower the gorge becomes until finally, direct sunlight can no longer reach its base. The rock too takes on an increasingly dark red colour. The effect on the visitor of passing through the Siq was no doubt experienced more intensely two thousand years ago. The traveller would have had several days of riding or walking through the desert behind him when he entered the corridor of rock leading to Petra. The deeper he penetrated into the Siq, the darker it became, in one spot the gorge becomes so narrow that it appears to close.

A few steps on, and the forty metre façade of the Treasury becomes visible through a crack where the Siq enters the valley (Figure 44). During the morning, the sun illuminates the colourful sandstone which reflects the sunlight in a range of reddish hues.

The sandstone rocks exhibit a variety of layered colours which, over different geological periods, have tilted and fractured to give the city its characteristic colouring. Since time immemorial the sand-laden desert winds have blown through the Siq and the rocks, sculpting and weathering them into fantastic shapes, which often make it difficult to distinguish where human work has begun, and nature's work has ended. Often, the forms created by nature over millenia are as intriguing and artistic as the architecture of Petra's classical period.

The path through the Siq

Even today, the walk to Petra can still be understood as an initiation in a metaphorical sense. The world of the senses becomes obscured and on all sides we are surrounded by bare, lifeless rock, giving the impression of impending death, but then, unexpectedly, like a vision, the Treasury rises before our eyes and we believe that we have woken in another world.

If we look in detail at the rock carvings and monuments in the Siq we can follow the transition from non-figurative to figurative depiction, which reflects the history and development of Nabatean religion. The first monuments which we encounter here are block monuments (Figure 42). These are large square blocks of stone, which mark the

Figure 44. The Treasury seen through the Siq.

places where an encounter with the spiritual and divine can take place, and are gigantic and permanent versions of smaller blocks which were carried by Nabatean caravan traders. Here they rest in all their glory, and probably belong to the earliest monuments of the city from the second century BC.

Even before we enter the Siq, three of these giant block monuments, of various sizes, can be seen to the right of the path. Their respective sites were probably determined by the most suitable rock formations. There can be no doubt, however, that the creators of these objects were driven by a clear purpose; like the smaller stone structures these creations marked a holy site, but here they are no longer in mobile format because this was a permanent settlement. Their huge size is also a mark of official recognition, as they can hardly be casual structures.

These block monuments might be seen as a first abstract depiction of a divine presence. A further development in the depiction of the divine can be seen in the relief niches found in the increasingly steep walls of the river bed. Here we find a depiction of three blocks, a larger central one surrounded by two smaller ones, like a faint echo of a trinity. Similar motifs of the trinity were depicted in many Nabatean sites in the Negev region which can be recognized by pottery findings as well as stone monuments at their edges. These consist of a larger stone in the middle (from 20 to 30 cm to more than 2 metres in size) accompanied on both sides by two smaller ones. No one today doubts the religious context of this combination of stones.[5]

In later monuments the abstract depiction is transformed to a tenuously recognizable face with eyes. Again and again the motif of the trinity appears in the grouping of three, at first in non-figurative steles, and later in steles with eyes.

A further step in the depiction of the deity is the monument in the form of an *obelisk* or *stele* (Figure 15). Here the cubic depiction of the divine presence is transformed into something that indicates a specific direction. The pillars, narrowing towards the top, point upwards. These also form the upper storey above a triclinium, and point in the direction in which the souls of the deceased who are commemorated in the triclinium can be encountered. We may assume that the lower

176

storey, the triclinium hewn into the rock, the interior space, was built or chiselled later than the upper part. The upper part is a metamorphosis of the cubic depiction of a divine presence, a presence which is already shown in its orientation towards the heavens. The power of the deity has changed from being in close proximity to distant transcendence.

Further along the course of the river bed we find, on leaving the Siq, mock structures (Figure 51) in which a small interior space which served religious purposes is dressed by a façade which is far larger than the interior space and which is crowned by a stepped motif. It depicts the stepped path which the human soul has to climb if it is to overcome the distance which has arisen between human beings and God in human consciousness. But it must strive to do so.

The monuments of Petra

The people who came to Petra at the time of the Nabateans were desert dwellers who visited the capital for religious reasons. Some of them, who had travelled to distant countries with their caravans, had seen similar monuments in India. However, the Nabatean style, which blended Egyptian and Greek stylistic elements with indigenous ones, must have appeared to them as something absolutely unique. Like most of the other rock monuments which can be found in the Petra area — they number more than a thousand — the Treasury was built in the years around the time of Christ.

The most striking buildings and works of stonemasonry in Petra are hewn into the rock. In contrast to more usual archeological sites in the Middle East, the remains of the past are largely exposed to view here. The works, chiselled into the rock, are much less exposed to decay and destruction than conventionally built works of architecture. As a result, the history of Petra's inhabitants has been engraved in stone as if in a symbolic language, and left to the modern visitor to decipher.

Past the Treasury, the valley becomes increasingly wider. Here too, the path is flanked by numerous rock monuments of various types. A road of columns modelled on the Roman style leads to temple which

Figure 45 (overleaf). Ed-Deir, popularly called the Monastery.   177

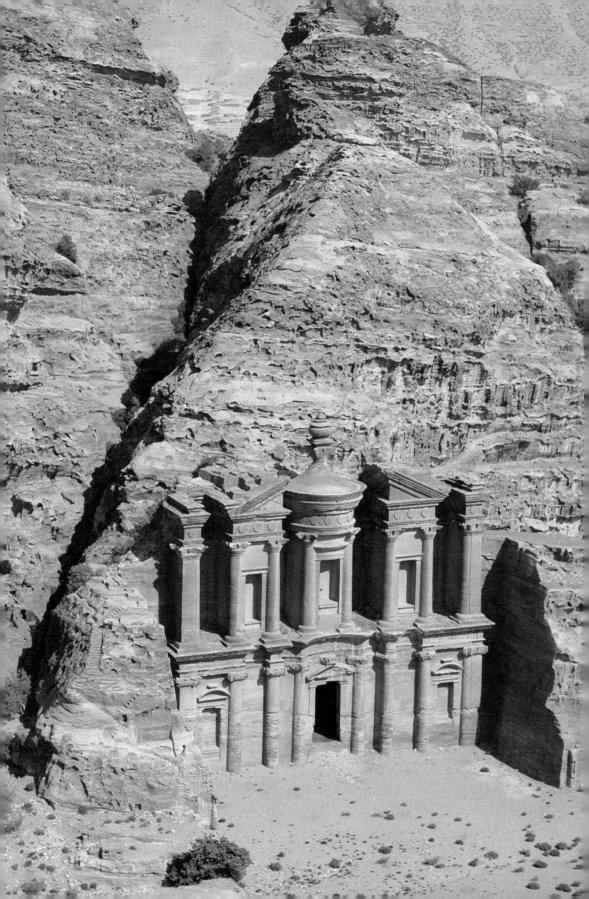

stands at the end of the valley in the shadow of a huge massif of rock (Figure 43). It is the temple of Dushrat, the main Nabatean god. From here where the valley opens out, it can only be left by steep paths which, following natural water courses, lead to other monuments, triclinia and places of sacrifice.

A few hundred metres after the Treasury, a path leads off to the left up a narrow valley. Various niches have been carved into the pink walls of rock. They are of different sizes, the smallest being approximately thirty to forty centimetres high, while the largest is approximately three metres (Figure 9). These relief niches mark places of divine presence. The latter is not yet depicted figuratively, but higher up the path the deity begins to be shown with the traces of a face. The transition can be seen in one of the *betyls* in Figure 12 (although that one is not from Petra). This path leads to the High Place, south of the centre of Petra.

On a high mountain top, more than one thousand metres above sea level and 150 metres above the river bed in Petra, this site is where sacrifices used to be held (Figure 8). It is all that remains from a time when animal sacrifices were still part of Nabatean cultic ceremonies. As well as the stone altars, again carved out of the solid surrounding rock, we can see basins for holding water, and the channels through which the blood of sacrifice drained away. However, animals were not the only things to be sacrificed, incense was also burned. The ceremonies took place in the open, and the rising smoke could be seen from the valley.

This early form of cultic ceremony was much admired and imitated by the people of Israel, but was something that the religious leadership sought to suppress. In contrast to Nabatean practice, in Judaism the religious cult was celebrated inside from the beginning, in which meant that it was accessible only to a leading priestly caste. In Judaism this completely open ceremony was seen as inappropriate from a very early stage onwards: 'But the high places were not removed; the people still sacrificed and burned incense on the high places ...' (2Kings 14:4). The Nabateans appear to have considered a public ceremony as something self-evident. Even in the Christian era, when the cultic ceremonies had moved completely inside, this public

Figure 46 (previous page). The Treasury, Petra.

*Figure 47.
The Greek god
Hermes-Mercury
with Semitic
features, Petra.*

aspect was still preserved. Access to the sacramental life was not re-
served to particular caste or tribe, but by a person's attitude. This attitude is reflected in the depiction of the deities which resemble Greek
or Roman gods with Middle Eastern Semitic features (Figure 47).

A further step towards a figurative depiction is the *betyl* from the
Temple of Petra (Figure 11). The deity already has a fully developed
face, and the Greek influence is very clear. in Greek culture, as we
know from their mythology, the gods were not a remote abstraction,
but could be encountered in human form. The deity was a being which
had become so well understood that it could be depicted in human
terms. This does not, however, mean that the earlier period, in which
stones marked the presence of a supersensory being, represented a less
developed state of soul. It reflected an attitude which did not need to
compress the supersensory into the sensory. This was a people who
had carried their gods as stone blocks through the desert for centuries,
and did not need worldly depiction of the divine. The same thing

181

Figures 49 & 50. Personification of spring and summer. Details from the mosaic floor of the Byzantine church in Petra.

applied to the children of Israel, who carried the Ark of the Covenant with them for forty years during the Exodus from Egypt. Attempts to move towards figurative depictions during the Exodus (such as the Golden Calf, Exodus 32) were strictly forbidden by one of the Ten Commandments. 'You shall not make for yourself a graven image ...' (Exod.20:4). Here, in Petra, such commandments were not imposed.

The taking of human form by the deity awoke a sense of inner space, both within and without human beings. Thus such spaces were created in Petra as well, initially taking the form of hollowed-out rock in which cultic acts were carried out.

Finally, the cultic ceremonies moved completely inside, which brings us to the *Qasr al bint* temple at the centre of the valley, (Figures 16 and 43). Here we find a fully enclosed temple, and unlike the hewn monuments it is built of stone blocks. It was built during the reign of Aretas IV shortly before the arrival of Christianity, and marks an important stage in the religious development from an outdoor nature religion to an inward and indoor personal religion. Within the wall which surrounds the whole of the building the sanctum is divided into three with a side length of approximately thirty-two metres. Parts

Figure 48. The 'Palace Tomb,' Petra.

of the building are decorated with blossom-like rosettes which are ordered in groups of three. We will see that this type of ornamentation was later refined in the churches of the Negev. The interior space of the sanctum is structured — here too there is the similarity with the later churches — with two rows each of six pillars, which divide the space into seven transverse bays. Thus seven spheres had to be passed through on the way to the altar. In Jerusalem this stage was reached with the building of the Temple of Solomon in the tenth century BC.

The anthropomorphic depiction of the deities is the last phase in Nabatean religion before the transition to Christianity. The divine world is experienced as being so close to human beings that it has taken human form. This is the last step before the depiction of a Son of God who combines the divine and the human. In recent years, a church from the Byzantine period was excavated in Petra. Here the stage had already been reached at which natural phenomena, such as, for example, the seasons, were personified (see Figures 49 and 50).

All depictions of the gods in the pre-Christian era were accessible to those who wanted to observe and worship. They were out in the open. Thus the course of development of Nabatean religious life was one which gradually led people — who initially strictly preserved their nomadic lifestyle — from religious ceremonies held under the heavenly vaults to the inside.

This is evident in different parts of the city as we have described. The early stage of outdoor sacrifice is visible in the high places of sacrifice (Figure 8). A second stage is represented by the Temple of Dushrat in the valley (Figures 16 and 43). Here sacrifices were initially performed on the roof; later, they were transferred to the inside of the building. The Temple of the Winged Lions at the northern edge of the river bed, is another example of the transition from outside to inside. In this area in which the church, mentioned above, was built — the final stage in the religious development of Nabatean culture before Islam took control in the seventh century.

The Treasury, standing at the entrance of the city of Petra is a masterpiece combining all the stages of Nabatean mythological consciousness in one: the threefold character of the former stone structures, relief motifs at the intermediate stage between figurative and non-figurative depiction, large interior spaces and *mock architecture,* and the illusion of inner space (Figures 44 and 46). What only became evident in a Greek temple once it was entered, is visible here from the outside. In the middle there is a niche containing a round tholos supported by four pillars almost completely filling the niche. The inner drum contains relief sculptures. Since this monument was worked out of the stone, static considerations could be left almost completely out of consideration.

At the far western end of the city a steep path hewn into the rock climbs up to a height of more than one thousand metres to the so-called *Monastery,* (Figures 28 and 45). This magnificent building, rivalling the Treasury, stands on a height from which there is a view far into Wadi Araba and across into the Negev desert. It is situated with a large open space in front which affords a better vantage point from which to study its splendour than the narrow cliff face from which one sees the Treasury. Here, too, we can see a combination of the stages of Nabatean religious history, The blind or silent rosettes are particularly visible above the second row of pillars. As mentioned earlier (page 121), these blossom forth into decorated rosettes in the Byzantine churches of the Negev.

For centuries, Bedouin who lived in this area kept strangers away from the city. They assumed that great treasures were hidden here which might be discovered and stolen by intruders. *Al-Khasneh Farun* means 'treasure of the Pharaoh.' When the first Europeans began to investigate Petra, any expectations of finding a 'treasure of the Nabateans,' foundered, for the treasures of this place do not consist of material riches; they are more valuable than that. It is the unique flowering of religious architecture which was more valuable by far than material riches.

No one can explain why this architectural period only lasted between seventy and ninety years, and why it ended as abruptly as it had begun. Another riddle is presented by the fact that this style can only be found in Petra and hardly anywhere else. Only the attempt to approach a solution to this issue by looking at the Nabatean way of thinking might give an insight to the heart of the riddle.

Petra as a religious centre

Petra gradually developed into the religious centre of the whole Nabatean region, and in the second century BC, it became the seat of the kings. The early places of sacrifice were placed on the mountains which surround the city on all sides. Over the course of one hundred and fifty years the rituals moved from the summits down into the temples of the city, from the open into an enclosed religious space. The majority of the Petran buildings which can still be seen today were built in the last two centuries before the end of the rule of the Nabatean kings in 106 AD, before Christianity could spread. Initially, these were simply 'dwellings of the gods.' Domestic buildings such as those which have been uncovered in more recent excavations, only arose later. Their number seems small when measured against the importance of this city and its size. Petra does not look as if it was a place which had a large number of permanent inhabitants.[6]

Petra occupied a special position as the capital of the Nabateans.[7] It was the residence of kings who devoted themselves mostly to spiritual affairs and religious practice rather than the daily affairs of politics. No royal palace has been found in Petra. The ruler was truly *primus inter pares,* first among equals. He lived among his people who gathered in Petra for religious events and set an example to them in their nomadic lifestyle. Neither prosperity nor immense political power could deflect the Nabatean kings from their traditional customs.

Mock architecture as expression of resurrection

Petra is usually described as a *necropolis,* a city of the dead. But anyone visiting Petra will find it hard to understand this, for it contradicts the feelings which arise when confronted with these ruined buildings.

From our study of the sparse historical records and the clues unearthed by archeologists, we can gain the impression that to the Nabateans, the physical and material world appeared as nothing more than an illusion; a corridor or anteroom to the world which was inhabited by the dead. There they awakened to new life as symbolized

Figure 51. The Carmine Tomb, Petra.   187

by the phoenix. The material world was like the desert which had to be journeyed through before one could reach Petra. Here, at the end of the pilgrim route, the link to the world after death was to be established through religious ceremonies with the assistance of the dead. This was the purpose of the numerous rock monuments. They cannot really be described as *buildings*. Despite the profusion of monuments, there is very little evidence of habitation. The pottery finds from Nabateans times are almost all characteristically delicate and fragile religious vessels, quite unsuited to everyday use.

The buildings sculpted out of the rock are restricted in their three-dimensional nature: They could never be free-standing; they are not quite appropriate for the material world; they are like illusions not wholly subject to the laws of matter. It is in line with this that they do not include spaces for religious ceremonies which would be appropriate in size for their external dimensions. In commemoration of the dead, kings and shepherds met in the darkness of the small interior spaces to undertake a ceremony which *removed all differences in rank.*

When the Nabateans became acquainted with Christianity, they underwent a change in thinking. Was it the result of St Paul's three year sojourn in Petra? For St Paul, the idea of the resurrection was a spiritual reality, not a physical and material one. Here in Petra there lived people for whom the connection with the dead, and the world of the hereafter, was also a certainty. The new faith, in which God came to human beings, must have fallen on fruitful soil here and been the fulfilment of everything already proclaimed in the old sun mysteries. The idea of the resurrection, which was already rooted in traditional Nabatean beliefs, spread an advent mood over the whole country which found fulfilment in Christ becoming human being. In a completely harmonious way the cross was recognized as the symbol of a new spirituality. This process must have started in Petra before gradually gaining ground in the whole of Nabatea.

It is perhaps an element of this profound spirituality which still speaks, on a deep, unconscious level, to the thousands of visitors today when seeing the ruins of Petra.

CHAPTER EIGHT

Shivta — City of Churches and Cisterns

Shivta is the Hebrew name commonly used for the ruined city which in the past was called *Sobota* or *Subeita* in Greek, and which, after its demise, was given the name *Isbeita* by the Arabs. It is the best-preserved classical settlement in the Negev and lies about forty kilometres south-east of Beersheba, in a region which has the lowest humidity. Its dryness is one of the reasons why the ruins have been so well preserved. Along with robbers, humidity is the greatest enemy of archeological remains.

The visitor reaches Shivta on a little-used road heading south from Beersheba through a region in which even today there are few settlements. Whereas Beersheba still belongs to the zone at the periphery of the desert where winter rainfall is just sufficient to allow agriculture without artificial irrigation, the measured annual rainfall in the vicinity of Shivta is less than one hundred millimetres — a value which is among the lowest in Israel (see Map 3). Water needs to be brought to the region from far away for cultivation of the fields. The closer one approaches Shivta from the north, the more the desert character of the landscape becomes apparent. The hills become more bare, and the vegetation poorer. Only a few species of plant can survive the lack of water during the long, dry summer months. No trees can cope with the heat and dryness. Only a few small-leafed bushes and grasses can thrive here. Nevertheless, visitors to the region of the northern Negev at the height of summer, can still see from the withered remains of

Figure 52. Partial three-dimensional reconstruction of the cityscape of Shivta (after A. Segal).

vegetation that spring covers the landscape with a thin fluff of grass. The further one penetrates to the south, the more sparse it becomes. Only in hollows in the ground is there sufficient moisture. Near Shivta only the dry beds of the wadis contain traces of plant life.

The proper road ends five kilometres from Shivta. From that point one reaches one's destination by desert track. The city lies in a valley

Figure 53. The Northern Church in Shivta with its three preserved apses.

which is about six or seven kilometres wide, the western side of which is furrowed by wide, sandy wadis while on the eastern side there is a gentle climb to the hills flanking the valley. Approximately in the middle of this valley, on the north side of Wadi Zeitan, there is a slight rise on which there are the ruins of the city of Shivta. More than a thousand years have passed since Shivta was abandoned by its inhabitants. Far distant from the most important transport routes, the place was hardly visited for many centuries and was spared deliberate destruction and over-building at a later time.

The rediscovery of Shivta

On approaching the city, the external walls and the apses of the Northern Church which open to the west, and which have been preserved to their full height, can be seen from a considerable distance. Shivta extends over an area of 81,000 square metres and did not possess a city wall as such. The external walls of the houses at the edge of the settlement form a closed stone shell which is broken only by a few access points. As the reconstruction diagram clearly shows (Figure 52), the layout of the city did not follow any regular shape. The outer boundary does not follow a regular line. In some places these outer walls have still been preserved to a height of four to five metres, and provide a rare opportunity to examine classical construction methods. The stones used come from the immediate vicinity of the settlement. The harder stones were used for the lower sections of the walls whereas softer limestone, which can easily be recognized by its smoother surface, was used for the upper storeys. At the highest point of the city, which falls away slightly to the south towards Wadi Zeitan, rise the still imposing remains of the Northern Church (Figure 53). Ruins of other large buildings can be found in the immediate vicinity of the settlement, such as communal wine presses, as well as large animal enclosures.

Although Shivta was one of the largest settlements in the Negev, even its former name was uncertain until the discovery of the papyri of Nessana during excavations between 1935 and 1937.[1] Documents dealing with military affairs do not even mention Shivta. The city was touched by none of the important routes through the Negev (see Map 2) and therefore clearly had no kind of military significance. Since it was not subject to threats of any kind and therefore did not possess any defences, it was probably not even classed as a city. Its mention in the papyri, which originated towards the end of the seventh century, is connected with donations to the monastery dedicated to St Sergius, and with complaints by its inhabitants about too high taxes under what was, at this point, already the Islamic regime. Whereas caravanserais were built on the sites of other former Nabatean settlements, Shivta, far away from the most-frequented caravan and trade routes, remained ignored for many centuries.

192

The scientific interest in this city began in 1904 with the archeological investigations of Vincent, Jaussen and Savignac. They discovered, among other things, an inscription on a stone which came from an older building and had been used in the construction of a church. It refers to King Aretas IV. The latter ruled from 9 BC to 240 AD. This means that the city must have been founded during the time of the Nabatean kingdom. Another inscription found outside the city which mentions the god Dushrat[2] also indicates the same period, as does Nabatean pottery found in the south of the settlement. It can be assumed that the place was inhabited long before this inscription was chiselled into the stone and the construction of stone houses began. Settlement of the hills of Shivta probably started in the first third of the first century BC. Why people should have chosen such a place, away from all the trade routes, which had no natural water resources apart from the winter rains, is still totally unclear. Settlement under these unfavourable conditions requires not only a good reason, but also a knowledge of how the desert can be tamed and made accessible to human civilization.

Secular buildings

In comparison to other Nabatean settlements, the construction of buildings was started relatively late in Shivta, namely in the years around the time of Christ. In the following centuries, the city expanded northwards from the banks of the Wadi Zeitan. The cityscape as we see it today bears typically Byzantine characteristics and dates from the fourth to sixth centuries. Earlier layers with traces of original Nabatean buildings, lie hidden under the ruins of later buildings in the southern part of the city and have not yet been excavated.

From the wadi, a road approximately two metres wide leads to the southern part of the city. If we enter Shivta at this spot, we see to our left a building whose walls have been preserved at a height of five metres (Figure 56). It is a characteristic example of the local Byzantine building style which is based on older Nabatean styles, and is rare for its state of preservation.[3] The collapsed northern wall allows us to

look into the interior, the ceiling of which is still largely intact, and was originally supported by three arches.

If we follow the road northwards for about one hundred metres, we come to a clearly recognizable city centre. It is a larger open square which was filled in earlier times by two large water reservoirs (Figure 57). One of them is only just recognizable. In contrast, the walls of the better preserved southern reservoir still contain traces of a water-tight lining. Some steps lead down into the basin and the stone channels, which carried a water from various directions into the reservoir, can also still be seen.

In planning the city, the natural lie of the land was used to catch the water of the few but heavy winter rainfalls. The roads were con-structed in such a way that the water flowed in stone channels directly into the central cisterns. In contrast to the typical look of a Roman set-tlement, in which the roads went in straight lines taking no account of the lie of the land, Shivta at first sight appears to be completely hap-hazard (see Figure 54), but this impression is deceptive. Each rise was taken into account to channel and collect water.

The Southern Church

East of the central water reservoir, we find the entrance to the atrium of the Southern Church (Figure 55). This belongs to the earliest Christian religious buildings in the Negev and therefore has many particular features which are no longer found in later church con-struction. Even today, the harmony of the building is still clearly vis-ible, and as a ruin the church still speaks a particularly pleasing language.

Three steps lead through a door, the frame of which is decorated with sculptures, into a small anteroom whose high ceiling was once supported by three transverse arches. To the left, there is another small room with a cistern. Before the water reached the collecting basin from the flat roof, it flowed through a siphon where any sand could be precipitated. Measured against the atriums of comparable church buildings, this anteroom is extraordinarily small (compare Figure 57). In planning the church — its construction was started

Figure 55. Southern Church, Shivta.

around the year 350, thus making it one of the oldest Christian monuments — account had to be taken of surrounding buildings. Whether this was the site of an earlier Nabatean shrine or even a temple, as is thought to be the case in Elusa, can only be discovered by further excavations. The dimensions of the actual space for the ritual had to accord with a strict order; this left the builders with no option but to make the anteroom smaller in order to fit the whole building into the available space, without destroying existing buildings and the water system.

As with all other churches in Shivta, the Southern Church also has an easterly orientation in the direction of the rising sun. The eastern end with its three apses remains almost undamaged to the present day (Figure 59). Only the central apse existed originally; the two sides apses were only added later. Inscriptions which were found in the

Figure 56. House at the southern wall, Shivta.

church indicate that the side apses were added towards the end of the fifth century. The transition to churches with three apses in the history of Christian church building thus took place in this church.[4] So far, there has not been any great success in finding an explanation for this transformation. What is certain, however, is that the language of forms of the space for Christian ritual, which receives the gaze of human beings into its threefold, semi circular sphere, represents more than a purely utilitarian purpose. The central apse rises to a considerable height, approximately seven metres, and the height of the side apses is about three and a half metres. Each of the side apses contains a semi-circular niche which repeats the gesture of the apse. The ground plan of apses comprises just over half a circular arch. This produces the impression of greater depth, thus emphasizing the enclosing gesture of this building element. It creates an impression of

198

Figure 57. City centre with Southern Church and public cistern.

seclusion in the observer in line with the feeling of inwardness which
was created in the soul of the faithful during the religious ceremony.
This design principle is also repeated in the other two churches in
Shivta, and represents an exception in the building style of the early
Christian churches in the Negev.

The walls of the apses consist of local stone like all the other

buildings and Shivta, and were given their final finish *in situ.*
Originally, the apses were colourfully painted inside. As late as the
early twentieth century, clear traces of these paintings could still be
seen. T. Wiegand, a German archeologist, was commissioned by the
Turkish military during the first world war, to provide a description of
the Negev and its ancient monuments. He wrote in his report, which
was published in 1920:

> Three figures were depicted in red, yellow and blue. The
> middle figure was long and upright with a nimbus. The figures
> on either side might be interpreted as angels flying towards the
> central figure or as adorers or apostles and the whole as the
> transfiguration of Christ or of Mary.[5]

The only thing that remains of all this today are a few bleached
remnants of red.

The main body of the Church is divided into a nave and two aisles.
The aisles are each separated from the nave by a row of columns. Six
columns on each side divide the space into seven transverse bays. If
we include the central apse, the total length of the church comes to
20.11 metres, with a width of 15.75 metres. The floor of the nave
originally consisted of marble slabs. The walls too were lined with
marble to about the height of a person, and it was put up at the same
time as the church was extended and the side apses were added.[6] This
grey marble was imported from Greece and transported through the
desert with some difficulty, given the restrictions on the weight that a
camel could carry. It was stolen in recent centuries; the bed of mortar
can still be seen in some places. Only a few small marble remains
bear witness to the magnificence of the interior decoration of this and
the two other early churches in Shivta.

Some of the remaining walls of the church are still standing at a
height of over two metres. Something of the protection and solemnity
which must have emanated from the room can still be felt today. Long
ago, these walls supported a tiled, wooden roof. In Elusa not far from
Shivta, fragments of tiles have been found near the church which was
partly excavated between 1979 and 1981, but only a few charred re-

Figure 58 Remains of the church of Elusa, the largest early-Christian basilica in the Negev, mid-fourth century. The bases of the marble pillars were found at their original sites.

mains which were discovered during excavations in the 1930s, are left of the wooden beams. Although in a considerably worse state of preservation than the churches in Shivta, the impression which is made by this religious space is no less impressive. Here the gaze of the visitor is drawn to the expanse of the desert landscape, emphasizing the polarity of experience of inner and outer (Figure 58).

All these churches were built at a time when the external form of a Christian religious building was not yet considered to be as important as it was to become in later times. It was only the inside which was thought through down to the smallest detail. A space was created for the congregation which had come to take part in the religious ceremony, providing an image of the inner processes through which the human soul passed during the sacraments. If the ancient pre-Christian

Figure 59 Eastern end of the Southern Church of Shivta with its three apses which are preserved to their full height.

Nabatean cults were such that they turned towards the stars and the forces in nature out in the open, the new Christian cult inaugurated an especially intimate soul and spiritual connection between human beings, as well as between human beings and the divine world. This occurred in the interior of the church, whose apses must be seen as the threefold image of the heavenly vaults. The contrast of life and death was reflected in the pre-Christian period, in the polarity represented by the expanse of the heavens and the open stage of the ritual on the one hand, and the experience of the interior of the earth, symbolized by the darkness of the spaces in the Petran tombs, on the other. The Christian religious ceremony required an interior space which merged these two archetypal principles through its shape. The ritual as ex-

Figure 60. Font in the Southern Church, Shivta.

pressed in the sacrament became an expression of the human soul aware of its own existence. The church façade is not at this early point, the subject of architectural and artistic attention. The external view of the church thus remained unobtrusive and was determined by the shape of the interior spaces and adjacent buildings.

In the Southern Church in Shivta there is a small, square room at the north end of the church which contains wall cupboards. These might have been used by the priests to keep the host as well as other ritual objects. Whether it was the vestry in which the priest prepared for the service or a chapel can no longer be determined with any certainty. Two rooms of small dimensions run parallel with the south wall of the church. One of them contained benches and in the neighbouring room there was an opening in the floor through which water could be drawn from a cistern. The existence of a water reservoir for religious purposes is another peculiarity of the Southern Church.

The public entered the church through the anteroom at the southeast corner of the building which we have already mentioned. The sculpting on the door lintel in symbolic language told the person entering of the events in which he was to participate during the course of the service.[7] A baptistery was attached to this space to the north and was entered by an anteroom at the south end. To the east it was concluded by an apse containing the stone font (Figure 60). This is shaped like a cross with interior dimensions of 1.70 x 1.38 metres, and a depth of 82 centimetres. Steps lead down in the western and eastern arm of the cross down which the person to be baptized went to be submerged. The basin consists of a single stone block which had to be worked on site. A block of this size which had already been hollowed out could no longer have been transported by the sixth century stone masons due to the brittleness of the soft stone. In earlier times, the basin would have been clad with marble slabs. They too were robbed but the holes for the dowels, the mortar bed and small fragments of marble provide evidence of their earlier existence. The size of the font indicates that it must have been intended for adults. It is only later in the history of Christianity that newborn infants were admitted to the community of Christians by means of baptism. A smaller, round basin which is also in this room might indicate that this transition took place as early as Nabatean times.

An area can be seen to the north of the baptistery of the Southern Church which served as a mosque. The *mihrab,* that typical prayer niche, was inserted in such a way that it took account of the construction of the neighbouring baptistery. If the Islamic invasion of the mid-seventh century signified the end for the rest of Byzantine-Nabatean civilization, both cultures appear to have continued to co-exist peacefully for a time in Shivta.

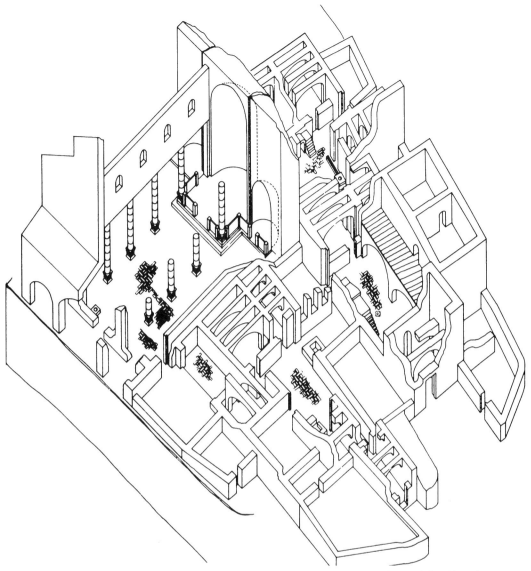

Figure 61. Attempted three-dimensional reconstruction of the Middle Church in Shivta and neighbouring buildings (after A. Segal).

The Governor's house and the Middle Church

A road with steps leads northwards from the Southern Church (Figure 62). Alongside it run stone channels and pipes, partly open partly, covered with stone slabs, which took the collected water to the central basins. The domestic buildings, of which nothing now remains except ruins, were built wall to wall. This meant that the total surface

Figure 63. So-called 'Governor's house,' Shivta.

< Figure 62. Steps leading from the 'Governor's house' down to the Southern Church, Shivta.

area of wall exposed to the sun could be reduced and the collection of the rain water which fell on the roofs was simplified. Part of the water was taken down the street to fill the communal reservoirs, while the other part was used to fill private cisterns in the buildings if they had any. It has to be remembered that rain could only be expected in the months from October to April and that the total rainfall in the year was less than four per cent of the annual average in central Europe. Although no other water was available, the city was nevertheless surrounded by extensive agricultural areas.

Domestic buildings as a rule possessed no courtyards or gardens.

Figure 64. Market place with Northern Church, Shivta.

Only a few exclusive houses had a patio which was presumably roofed. The close proximity of the buildings in the city was relieved by generous and well thought-out squares. If we follow the road we have just mentioned, we reach such a square. It is dominated by the façade of a house which was described as the *Governor's house* by an expedition headed by an American named Colt in the 1930s (Figure 63). It is one of the few houses in which the ceiling of the first storey, consisting of stone slabs, and the second storey above it can still be seen in their original state.

The smallest and most recent of the three churches in Shivta is situated a little further to the north directly next to this house (Figure 61). It was built during the sixth century in a part of the city where settlement had already occurred, and had to be adapted to the existing buildings. This can be seen from its proximity to the road, the absence

Figure 65. Atrium and main building of the Northern Church, Shivta.

of the atrium and the very small narthex. The section of road in front of the entrance was given a special surface which was not otherwise used in road construction. If the building near it really was the Governor's house, we might conclude from this that the church served as a religious building for the members of the city administration who had converted to Christianity at an early stage. This would also explain why, in contrast to the other churches in Shivta, there is no baptistery here.

The columns of the Church were donated by the citizens of the city in commemoration of the dead. Their names, as the inscriptions show, display an interesting combination of Nabatean and Greek elements. Take the Nabatean name *Wail* for instance, which turned into *Ouaelos* and can be seen in Greek writing on a capital of one of the pillars of this church: 'For the redemption and peace of Ouaelos, son of

Zonainos ...'[8] The existence of Graecized names indicates that Nabatean traditions continued to exist for as much as half a millennium after the Negev had become part of the Roman Empire. The occurrence of Nabatean names is a sure sign that a large part of the population which lived here until the seventh century was of direct Nabatean descent, and indicates, like many other features, that the dissolution of the Nabatean kingdom and the transition to Christianity, were phases in an organic process and did not result in sharp caesuras. New impulses were able to take effect in total harmony with existing traditions. The old Nabatean names were still in use although the Greek language had in the meantime become dominant.

The Northern Church

Through a cobbled square we reach the third largest church complex of Shivta on the northern edge of the city (Figure 64). The largely preserved external wall of the church, once the largest building in the city, forms a part of the external shell which surrounded the whole settlement. Originally it was probably a monastery church which was built at the same time as the Southern Church at the end of the fourth century, in an area which at that time still lay outside the city limits.

Before entering the body of the church, there is a spacious atrium (Figure 65). It is surrounded by several smaller rooms which belong to the monastery complex. Christianity spread in the south of the Holy Land largely through the presence of monks and hermits. Their agricultural and craft activities, which were able to develop in the monasteries, resulted in increasingly large numbers of people settling in their surroundings. However, the spiritual life which developed here also promoted the influx of a growing number of people of the Christian faith. Thus in Shivta, too, the construction of the city is likely to have encroached increasingly on the monastery area until it was assimilated completely within the city walls.

Initially, the Northern Church probably mainly served the inhabitants of the monastery for religious practices and meditation. The design of the interior space corresponds largely with that of the

Figure 66. Screen pillar from the fourth century, buried under the bema during redevelopment of the Northern Church in the sixth century and discovered by the author in 1992.

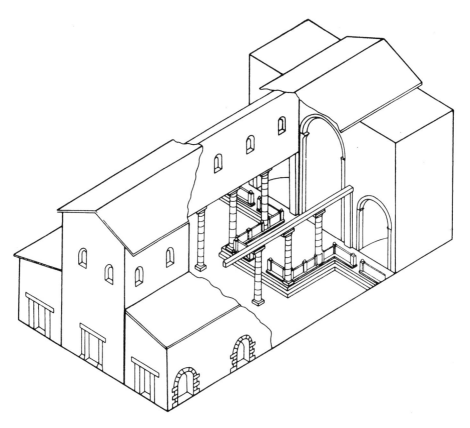

Figure 67. Attempted reconstruction of the Northern Church in Shivta (after R. Rosenthal-Heginbottom)

Southern Church. It is a basilica with a nave and two aisles, with two rows of six columns which here too, divide the main body of the church into seven transverse bays. The dimensions of the space are also roughly equal to those of the Southern Church. It is somewhat longer at twenty-two metres but also narrower. The position of the pulpit between the third and fourth columns of the northern aisle can still be clearly seen today. In the Northern Church the three apses are also still fully preserved. The height of the central apse is 8.5 metres, the side apses are 4.25 metres high. Again the two side apses each have a semi-circular niche which emphasizes the language of forms of the eastern end and its threefold principle. The vaults of all three domes are divided from the wall by a projection, thus emphasizing the individual shapes as independent construction elements.

To begin with, the first building phase was thought to have started towards the end of the fourth century, shortly after the construction of the Southern Church had begun. However, excavations from 1985, indicate that there were numerous changes to the interior. So, two construction phases can be distinguished in the *bema* (Hebrew: platform), the raised area surrounding the altar or sanctuary. During reconstruction of the church at the end of the fifth century, possibly connected with the enlargement of the monastery, the interior of the church was lined with Greek marble and expanded by the two side apses, like the other churches in the city. A space was opened behind the end wall of the southern aisle and given a vault, thus transforming it into a side apse. This happened at the same time that numerous new churches were being built everywhere in the Negev in order to meet the growing Christian religious requirements of the population. The original and much more modest decoration from the fourth century was only uncovered by later excavations. The religious elements of the older interior were buried under the enlarged bema during rebuilding, including parts of the choir screen which separated the bema from the lay area, as well as a pillar of the screen which it is possible to date to the fourth century (Figure 66). It is decorated with typically Nabatean diagonal hatching. All these older finds consisted of local soft limestone and only remained so well preserved because they were buried for centuries in the earth.

The earliest Christian inscription found in Shivta was dated the year 505. Since being transcribed, it has been lost and its exact location can only be guessed at, but its wording indicated that it related to the completion of the extension and reconstruction work on the church: 'By God's help this work was completed during the time of the most enlightened prior and during the time of Flavius Johannes, son of Stephen, the vicar.'

A new period of religious life began. The intimacy of modest houses of God was replaced by richly decorated churches which took in not only the inhabitants of the place but also pilgrims on the way to the distant Sinai, to Mount Moses. During this period, in which increasingly large numbers of people gathered for the Christian service, the reliquary cult also began. In its early form it belonged to the

Figure 68. House cistern with pipe and water basin, Shivta. Rope marks can still be seen at the edge of the cistern opening. The inside of the pipe through which the water reaches the cistern has the typical Nabatean grooved pattern.

special features of Nabatean Christianity, and can be considered as a continuation and transformation of the pre-Christian cult of the dead.

At the start of the sixth century, an earthquake brought the church close to collapse. The outer walls were strengthened and provided with filling, as is evident from the only partly smoothed stones. This thick stone mantle is two metres wide at its base and has been preserved in part to a height of 4.5 metres, giving the building the look of a castle or fortress. To the present day, it has largely fulfilled its task of preventing the church from collapsing. The relatively rough working of the stones contrasts sharply with the care with which the walling behind it had been treated.

Towards the end of the same century, members of the congregation began to be buried within the church. In the Northern Church there were eighteen Greek tomb inscriptions from the years 595 to 679. There is a baptistery as well as an additional chapel with a semi-circular apse, which is attached to the external southern wall of the church. The font in the baptistery, just like the one in the Southern Church, is of a size which clearly indicates the baptism of adults. In the sixth century, when a large number of people found their way to Christianity, a single baptistery no longer appeared to be sufficient in Shivta.

Cityscape and domestic architecture

In the square in front of the church (Figure 64), where the market might have been held in earlier times, there are several adjoining houses which served as workshops. Thus an oven can still be seen there which might have belonged to a bakery or pottery. There are also the remains of a wine press. The surface on which the grapes would have been trodden with bare feet still exists as well as the channels by which the juice would have flowed into a basin below. The latter has the typical diagonal hatching of Nabatean cisterns on its walls. There were two other grape crushing and pressing facilities in the east and west of the city. Only a significant harvest of grapes can explain the construction of three such facilities.

Near the Northern Church there are also the ruins of larger domestic dwellings with several rooms. Their windows are tiny in order to prevent the entry of direct sunlight during the summer and the escape of heat in the winter. All buildings in Shivta were built of stone; their external walls were relatively thick, consisting mostly of several layers, thus providing good insulation. Many buildings had two storeys and some of them even had a cistern of their own with a depth of four to five metres into which water was channelled during the short rain period, by means of stone pipes (Figure 68). There were few decorative elements; some of the more exclusive houses sometimes had mosaic floors.

A typical domestic dwelling in Shivta consisted of a large entry hall below which was usually the house cistern. In some cases this space was also arranged as an open inner courtyard from which the living quarters could be accessed. Door lintels and sills were often decorated. The roofs of the houses consisted of stone slabs which were supported by masonry arches (Figures 20 and 25). Wood was only used as a building material in these desert cities for public buildings, and had to be transported over long distances. It was needed to provide roofing for spaces whose areas were too large to be bridged by arches made of relatively soft limestone. This construction method produced a cityscapee which was dominated on the one hand, by the straight lines and right angles of the buildings, and on the other hand, by the semi-circular forms of stone arches which typically governed the look of the living spaces, and which could also be seen at the many gates and doors of the city. For more than seven hundred years the life of people was accompanied by the sound of masonry tools. The marks of notched chisels can still be seen to this day.

The surrounding area of Shivta

If we approach Shivta on the path described earlier, we come past a rock outcrop which guards entry to the valley. From its height one has a view of the whole valley with its dry wadis and the ruins of this formerly thriving city. The hill, which towers above Shivta by about eighty metres, consists at its highest point of a flat area surrounded by a wall which narrows towards the east in the direction of the valley. It is about 120 metres long and its average width is about thirty metres. On the north slope there are several cisterns which supplied the rural population of the surrounding areas with water.

The remains of what is thought to have been a bell tower were found on the south-eastern edge of the slope.[9] Several small rooms, each with a well preserved stone bench as well as a niche hewn into the stone wall, are situated on the southern slope. The openings of these rooms, which are spanned by arches, provide a view along the wide valley as far as Shivta. On the plateau there is the apse of a chapel (Figure 69) and the foundation walls of a larger building with one main room and four side rooms. The area was bounded by a wall on the western, wider side of the slope, and access was provided by a gate.

216

Figure 69. Apse of a chapel which is thought to have belonged to a shrine of St George, Mashrafe near Shivta.

A partly buried, arch-like opening in the rock marks the entrance to the subterranean part of the complex. The hidden passageways, partly bricked and partly hewn into the rock, can only be accessed by crawling. Greek inscriptions and symbols have been scratched into the walls. Many of them have not been deciphered to this day, but one of them gives the name of St George. Several of the underground rooms are still completely preserved. It is thought that there is another basement storey below them which has not yet been investigated. There are clear signs that part of the complex near to the eastern slope was destroyed by an earthquake. Some of the damaged buildings were reconstructed at a later time.

Mashrafe is the name given by the Bedouin to these ruins. There are no other more exact indications as to the identity of this place. Only thorough excavations can produce further information. The curious discoveries include three circles made of chiselled stone, providing an indication of the religious significance of this place. It is as if a former Nabatean site of the sun cult had developed here into a spiritual centre of Christianity. There can be little doubt that this was an important monastery complex. An Italian by the name of Anthony of Piacenza, who travelled through the Negev in 570, describes a monastery with a guest house ten miles distant from Elusa and a church dedicated to St George.[10] The city of Shivta, however, is not mentioned by him. Yet there is some justification in assuming that this is the place he referred to. The mention of a guest house provides evidence of a significant flow of pilgrims who either rested here on their journey to the Sinai, or whose objective was the monastery itself as a place to venerate the saint.

Monastery life at that time combined two contradictory tendencies of religious behaviour. On the one hand, there was inner contemplation, withdrawal from the world and the endless expanse of the desert into the security of the monastery cell. On the other hand, there was the intentional subjugation to the strict regime of the monastery community in order to do justice to the contemporary ideas about a life pleasing to God. Such monastic communities could quickly turn into the religious, cultural, and economic centres of a whole region. The agricultural areas of the city of Shivta extended to the foot of the hill. We can assume that it formed a kind of stronghold of spiritual life for the city. In turn, the proximity to a settlement ensured a vital link with the external world for the monastery's inhabitants, while still preserving the necessary distance for them to live a strictly religious life.

Religious customs and participation in the Christian sacrament were of central importance for the inhabitants of the Negev in the Byzantine age. Shivta, as a place off the beaten track, which presumably only maintained sporadic contact with other cities, appears to have developed its own culture with its own particular characteristics, as well as very specific religious practices. The reciprocal inspiration of city and religious centre is one of those special characteristics.

Map 5. Trade routes of the ancient world.

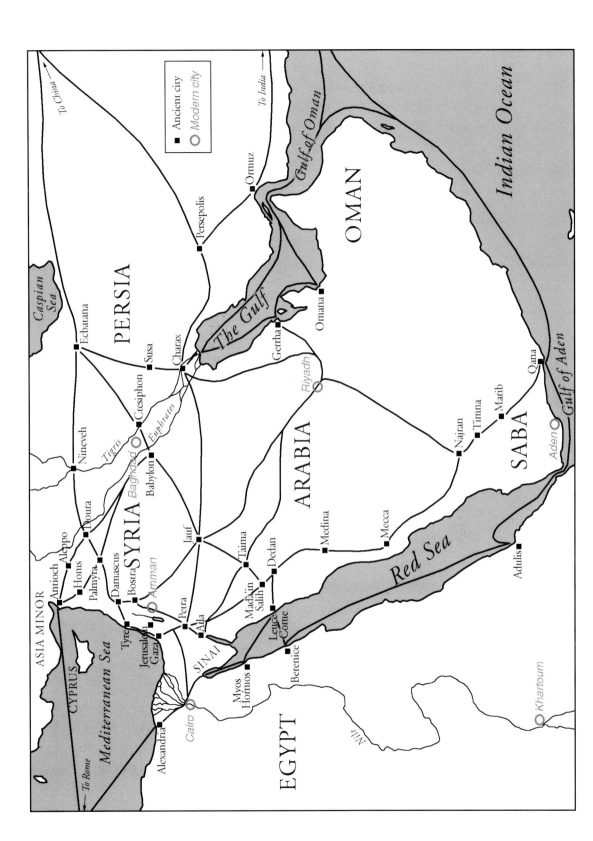

An encounter with the past

An account of Shivta which attempts to convey something of the magic of this city cannot finish without reproducing the very personal statement of an archeologist who has contributed more than anyone else to preventing Nabatean civilization from being forgotten. In his book *Temple, Kirchen und Zisternen (Temples, Churches and Cisterns),* Avraham Negev describes the following experience:

> During one of my first visits to Sobota in 1944, I approached the cobbled square in front of the church. It was a very hot Chamsin day (Chamsin = hot desert wind) but now the pitiless sun was about to sink. A light Mediterranean breeze made it easier to breathe. There was a profound silence and the only sound was the faint chirping of the crickets. In the shadow of the high wall I saw some scribbles on the cobbles, faint lines of a game which children have played from time immemorial. It was as if I could still hear the sound of the game counters. Suddenly I became aware of the quiet shuffling sound of bare feet on the cobbles and the sound of little bells, and I could smell the scent of incense. It was so real that I did not dare to raise my eyes to see the slow procession of white-robed priests into the basilica. — If there were ever a kind of 'ordination' for archeologists, that was the moment when it would have happened for me.[11]

Conclusion

Perhaps something of the mystery of the Nabateans has been descried in these pages. They stand out from all other ancient civilizations for three particular qualities which we might strive for, even today. Firstly, their independence, which was based on uncommon political skill in avoiding armed conflict wherever possible. Secondly, they had a remarkable facility to assimilate influences from other cultures and yet produce something uniquely their own. Finally, they showed a continual ability to enrich and transform their culture in an extraordinary development, from invisible beginnings to highly sophisticated, refined results.

However, despite contemplating the ruins of their long-forgotten civilization, we are left with more questions than answers, and can but discern an echo a mirage of the life hidden beneath the timeless desert sands.

Appendix

Chronology

General historical dates relating to the northern Arabic and Judean region:

25000–4000 BC	Stone age
4000–3100	Chalkolithicum
3100–1200	Bronze age
1200–1000	Iron age
1000–900	Kingdom of Israel
900–586	The kingdoms of Israel and Judea
586	Fall of the Israelite-Judean kingdom
586–332	Persian period
332–152	Greek period
152–37	Maccabean period
37 BC – 4 AD	Herod the Great
70	Destruction of the 2nd Temple of Jerusalem
70–324	Roman period
324–638	Byzantine period
638–1099	Arabic-Islamic period
1099–1291	Time of the Crusades

The main Nabatean sites

Nabatean history takes place around Wadi Araba, south of the Dead Sea. Petra lies to the east hidden on the high plateau of Edom in Jordan, while to the west in Israel are the cities of the desert in the Negev.

Avdat [Greek: *Oboda, Eboda;* Arabic: *'Abdeh*]

Avdat is situated on a ridge rising some 70–80 m over the surround plain in the Negev, about 650 m above sea level. As a city Avdat has a special place. The Nabatean acropolis is a completed architectural monument. While it was originally a caravanserai, the change to a city is clear. There are ancient potteries to be seen, an underground necropolis, and (as in most of the other cities) the remains of churches to be seen.

The site is open to the public and includes a visitor centre with a small museum and a video show giving a flavour of the life of the original inhabitants.

Mampsis [Hebrew: *Mamshit;* Arabic: *Kurnub*]

Mampsis lies in the Eastern Negev by Wadi Mamshit. It is the easternmost settlement of the Negev and grew out of a caravanserai on the frankincense route. The Greek name, Mampsis, can be found on the Madaba mosaic map of the seventh century (see Figure 26). Here, too, there are churches and baptismal fonts to be seen which are decorated with mosaics which have survived. About fifty houses in various conditions, as well as parts of the city walls can be seen. Extensive stables were excavated, and frescoes decorating a brothel were found. The buildings of the British Mounted Police constructed during the British Mandate (1919–48) from the stones of the ruins, have been converted to 'Nabatean restaurant' named after the Nabatean goddess Dushura.

Elusa [Hebrew: *Khaluza;* Arabic: *Khalassah*]

Elusa (or Elousa) lies in the very easternmost area of Sarah sand deposits. Only the finest of wind-blown sands are blown this far on the prevailing west winds. The area of the city is extensive lying between two wadis and has hardly been excavated. The largest church in the Negev (partly excavated) and a free-standing theatre are the only buildings which are visible. Most of the cities lies under the desert dunes. The oldest Nabatean inscription was found here (Fig. 6).

Elusa can only be reached by four-wheel drive vehicles and needs local knowledge to find.

Ruheiba [Hebrew: *Rechovot;* Greek unknown; Arabic: *Ruheiba*]

Ruheiba, about 12 km south of Elusa, has only been partly explored. Three large churches including one with an underground crypt — perhaps a place of pilgrimage — have been identified, but there may be more. The quality of secular architecture is very high. Several deep wells were dug in Byzantine times, up to 80 m deep.

The latest archeological excavations took place some years ago and all the results have not yet been published. The site is in a nature conservation area and can only be visited by agreement of the authorities.

Nessana [Hebrew: *Nitzana;* Arabic: *'Ujah al-Khafir*]

Nessana has a church built on the highest part of the town, probably on the site of an earlier Nabatean acropolis. First excavations took place in the 1930s when the papyri discussed earlier were discovered. They were in a room adjoining the church. During the past decades further excavations uncovered different parts of the town. Unfortunately they have not been up to the usual high standards of today — some 'loci' are not covered over again, resulting in deterioration. The results of the work have not been published.

However, Nessana is well worth a visit. It is easily reached (very close to the Israel-Egypt border), and one usually has the site to one-self, allowing the atmosphere of the desert to be absorbed un-disturbed.

Mada'in Salih

Like Petra, Mada'in Salih has buildings carved out of the solid rock. It is in northern Saudi Arabia, and cannot at present be visited by western tourists.

There are numerous other small unexcavated sites in the Araba Valley, the Negev, Jordan and Saudi Arabia.

References

Chapter 1

1 A. Musil, *Arabia Petraea.*
2 A. Negev, *Land of the Negev,* I, p. 227ff.

Chapter 2

1 See A. Negev, *Masters of the Desert,* p. 34.
2 See Josephus, *Antiquities,* 14.
3 We will cite just one of the many sources here: G. Mandel, *Il regno di Saba.*
4 See E. Yassif, *Tales of Ben Sira.*
5 G. Mandel, *Il regno di Saba.*
6 See Josephus, *Antiquities* 11.325–39, as well as Talmud, Joma, 69a.
7 Diodorus, *History,* 2.48.
8 Diodorus, *History,* 2.48.
9 Diodorus, *History,* 19.97.
10 Diodorus, *History,* 19.94.
11 See A. Negev, *Masters of the Desert.*
12 See H.K. Beebe, *The Dromedary Revolution.*
13 Strabo, *Geographica,* XVI 4,26.
14 A. Jaussen, R. Savignac and H. Vincent, 'Abdeh,' *Revue Biblique* 13, 1904/1905.
15 See A. Negev, 'Personal Names.'
16 More detailed information in R. Wenning, 'Eine neuerstellte Liste der nabatäischen Dynastie,' in *Boreas, Münstersche Beiträge zur Archäologie,* Volume 16, Münster 1993.
17 See p. 53 and A. Negev, 'Personal Names.'
18 Strabo, *Geography,* 16.4.26.
19 For further details concerning this transition process see pp. 95 and 101.
20 See P. Figueras, 'The Christian History of the Negev and Northern Sinai, Tantur Papers on Christianity in the Holy Land,' in Jaeger, *Christianity in the Holy Land.*
21 See R. Rubin, *The Negev as a Settled Land,* p. 61f.

Chapter 3

1 Rudolf Steiner suggests this process began among the ancient Hebrews with Abraham, evolved gradually up to the Mystery of Golgotha, and thereafter developed also within other groups of peoples. See, *Deeper Secrets of Human History,* particularly the lecture of November 9, 1909.
2 For the evolution of consciousness see Rudolf Steiner in *Cosmic Memory* and *An Outline of Esoteric Science* as well as *World History.*
3 R. Steiner, *Mystery Knowledge,* lecture of December 22, 1923, p. 180.
4 A. Cruden, *A Complete Concordance,* p. 325.

5 Compare also p. 92ff for the importance of Pauline Christianity for the Nabataeans.

6 See D. Flusser, *Jewish Sources in Early Christianity*. The essay 'The Origins of Christianity in Judaism' in particular contains several references to this crossover.

7 H. Jonas, *The Gnostic Religion,* p. 34.

8 Compare J. Ryckmans, *L'institution monarchique*. Concerning the origins of Nabataean civilization in the southern Arabian region compare also: R. Kutzli, *Die Bogumilen,* p. 108, as well as G. Mandel, *Il regno di Saba.*

9 Compare P. Rost, *Die Keilschrifttexte Tiglat-Pilesers.*

10 See reference to 'Saba' in *Biblical Lexikon.*

11 See reference to 'Arabien' in *Biblical Encyclopedia,* p. 352.

12 Stephen, *Ethnica.*

13 Strabo, *Geographica.*

14 See F. Zayadine, 'Die Götter der Nabatäer,' p. 115.

15 Maximus, *Philosophoumena.*

16 *Suda Lexicon.*

17 There is a detailed explanation of these idols in J. Patrich, 'Prohibition of a Graven-Image.'

18 Joseph Patrich provides the most detailed presentation of the so-called non-figurative tendency in Nabataean art, which was, of course, strictly subordinated to religious functions.

19 N. Glueck, *Deities and Dolphins.*

20 See, for example, N. Glueck, *Deities and Dolphins.*

21 A. Negev, *Masters of the Desert,* p. 232. For further details about the 'secondary' Nabataean deities compare also F. Zayadine, 'Die Götter der Nabatäer,' p. 113ff.

22 Compare A. Negev, 'Greek Inscriptions.'

23 Stephen, *Ethnica.*

24 Epiphanios, *Panarion.* 22.9–12.

25 A. Negev, *Masters of the Desert,* p. 231

26 See also A. Negev, *Masters of the Desert,* p. 232. The author is of the same view.

27 Compare F. Zayadine, 'Die Götter der Nabatäer' in M. Lindner *Petra.* p. 116ff.

28 The inscription is dated to the year 9 AD and is published in F. Rosenthal, *Aramäistische Forschung.*

29 A. Negev, *Masters of the Desert,* p. 231.

30 See Rudolf Steiner, *Theosophy.*

31 A detailed treatment of the East-West problem in connection with the emergence of Gnosticism in H.M. Gwatkin, *Early Church History,* Vol. II, p. 19ff.

32 The author holds the view that anthropological investigation of remains in Nabataean graveyards could produce astonishing results in this field and substantiate this assumption.

33 Particularly in A. Negev, 'Petra.'

34 A. Negev, *Masters of the Desert,* p. 88.

35 See O. Murray, *Sympotika.*

36 Strabo, *Geographica,* 16.4.26.

37 R. Brünnow and A. v. Domaszewski, *Provincia Arabia Petraea,* Vol. I.

38 F. Zayadine, 'Die Felsenarchitektur Petras,' p. 124ff.

39 F. Zayadine, 'Die Felsenarchitektur Petras,' p. 133.

40 Compare also H. Leicht, *Kunstgeschichte der Welt.*

41 Concerning the rock shrines in India see H. Rau, *Stilgeschichte der indischen Kunst.*

42 A. Negev, 'Excavations at Elusa.'

43 J. Licht, *The Rule Scroll.*

44 Strabo, *Geographica,* 16.4.26.

45 *Jerusalem Talmud,* Ch. 1, Roll XIV.

46 See A. Smallwood, 'High Priests and Politics,' as well as Josephus *Antiquities,* 18.2.2.

47 See R. Steiner, *Building Stones,* lecture of March 27, 1917.

48 See P. M. Allen, *Christian Rosenkreutz Anthology.*

49 S. von Gleich, *Marksteine der Kulturgeschichte,* p. 144ff.

50 S. von Gleich, *Marksteine der Kulturgeschichte,* p. 150ff. Concerning the pre-Christian phoenix mysteries see also R. van den Broek, *The Myth of Phoenix,* pp. 307 and 394ff.

51 See Ph. Schaff and H. Wace, *Nicene and Post-Nicene Fathers.*

52 R. Steiner, *Karmic Relationships,* Vol. II, lecture of April 27, 1924, p. 83.

53 See also pp. 196f and R. Rosenthal-Heginbottom, *Die Kirchen von Sobota,* p. 203ff.

54 See K. Heussi, *Der Ursprung des Mönchtums.*

55 See L. Casson and E.L. Hettich, *Excavations at Nessana,* Vol. II.

Chapter 4

1 M. Avi-Yonah and Y. Yadin, *Six Thousand Years of Art,* pp. 216–21.

2 This is also the opinion of Abraham Negev in a unpublished essay, *Iconoclastic Nabataean Style.*

3 See A. Negev, *Masters of the Desert,* p. 175 ff.

4 See J. Shereshevski, *Byzantine Urban Settlements in the Negev Desert,* p. 149ff.

5 See A. Negev, 'Die Töpferwerkstatt in Oboda (Avdat).'

6 K. Schmitt-Korte, 'Die bemahlte nabatäische Keramik,' p. 205ff.

7 Pliny, *Epistelarum,* 10.40.

8 R. Steiner, 'Essence and Task of Freemasonry from the Point of View of Spiritual Science,' in *The Temple Legend,* lecture of December 2, 1904.

9 The exact percentage of the population which was literate is unknown. Estimates vary between 4% and 10% in Judea at the time of the birth of Christ. As explained on p. 143, it might have been higher among the Nabataeans, but still very low by today's standards.

10 In pre-Christian times, a kind of 'sky burial' took place as is still customary among Indian Parsees. The corpse was laid out in the desert where it rapidly decomposed or was removed by birds of prey and wild animals. The urbanization process made such burial practices increasingly impossible.

11 This inspired N. Glueck to call his book *Deities and Dolphins.* For further information concerning the early Christian language of symbols see E. Ringel, *Das Urchristentum.*

12 See A. Kasher, *Edom, Arabia and Israel,* p. 21, as well as the literature mentioned there.

13 Josephus *Jewish Wars,* 7.8.7.

14 See for example H. Rau, *Stilgeschichte der indischen Kunst,* pp. 25 and 45.

15 See V. Tzaferis, *Christian Symbols.*

Chapter 5

1 Diodorus, *History,* 19.94.

2 Strabo, *Geographica,* 16.4.26.

3 Diodorus, *History,* 19.99.

4 Pliny, *Natural History,* 12.30ff.

5 See H.K. Beebe, *The Dromedary Revolution.*

6 See Y. Meshorer, *Nabataean Coins,* p. 67.

7 Strabo, *Geographica,* 16.4.26.

8 A. Negev, *Nabatean Cities,* p. 16.

9 Estimates of the extent of this area vary a great deal. This figure is not the highest. It is taken from A. Negev, *Masters of the Desert,* p. 205. Another very informative study is contained in Y. Kedar, *Ancient Agriculture.* That, however, refers to 4,000 square kilometres.

10 Research into agriculture in the Negev in classical antiquity has largely been undertaken by Israeli academics. We will mention just one source here which, apart from a detailed exposition, also contains further references: Evenari, Shanan and Tadmore, *The Negev.*

11 See Y. Kedar, *Ancient Agriculture,* p. 47.

Chapter 6

1 Stephen, *Ethnica.*

2 Numerous examples of this in A. Negev, 'The Inscriptions of Wadi Haggag.'

3 The Finnish *Kalevala* epic, for instance, was written down by E. Lönnrot for the first time in the mid-nineteenth century.

4 See Diodorus, *History,* 2.48.

5 Josephus, *Contra Apion,* 1.12.

6 The Nabataean script appears in its earliest archaic form in the second century BC; see p. 50.

7 See A. Negev, *The Inscriptions of Wadi Haggag.*

8 With reference to the demonization of the Queen of Sheba see E. Yassif, *Tales of Ben Sira.*

9 Smith, George Adam, *The Historical Geography of the Holy Land.,* p. 318f.

10 Diodorus, *History,* 19.94.

11 See Joshua 3:10: 'And Joshua said, "Hereby you shall know that the living God is among you, and that he will without fail drive out from before you the Canaanites, the Hittites, the Hivites, the Perizzites, the Girgashites, the Amorites, and the Jebusites".'

12 See for example Lev.19:33f; Deut.16:14; Jeremiah 14:8.

13 See J. Shereshevski, *Byzantine Urgan Settlements.*

14 See A. Segal, *Architectural Decoration in Byzantine Shivta.*

15 A. Segal, *Architectural Decoration in Byzantine Shivta,* p. 156.

16 See A. Negev, *Land of the Negev,* the chapter on 'Nabateans in the Negev.'

17 A. Negev, 'Personal Names.'

18 A. Kasher also refers to these links, which extended as far as India, in *Edom, Arabia and Israel.*

19 Diodorus, *History,* 2.48.

20 Strabo, *Geographica,* 16.4.21

21 Ch. Clermont-Ganneau, *Recueil d'archeologie Orientale.*

22 See Y. Meshorer, *Nabataean Coins,* p. 86.

23 Josephus, *Jewish Wars,* 1.7.8.

24 Strabo, *Geographica,* 16.4.21.

25 Further details about the life and work of Syllaeus in M. Lindner, *Petra,* pp. 65ff.

26 Shallum, the son of Jabesh, who only ruled Israel for one month (2Kings 15:13).

27 Strabo, *Geographica,* 16.4.26.

28 See Stephen, *Ethnica.*

29 See R. Steiner, *Egyptian Myths and Mysteries; Cosmic Memory* and *The Fifth Gospel.*

30 Talmud, *Massechet Avot* (Chapter of the Fathers), 1. The text was codified about 200 AD and has remained unchanged from that time onwards, like the rest of the Talmud. The term 'Torah' comprises the Ten Commandments, but in a metaphorical sense also the word spoken by God.

Chapter 7

1 J.L. Burckhardt, *Travels in Syria.*

2 P.J. Parr, 'Vierzig Jahre Ausgrabungen in Petra' in M. Lindner, *Petra,* pp. 195ff.

3 Diodorus describes Petra (Sela) as the place of refuge of nomadic Nabataeans *(History,* 19.95).

4 This only happened with Solomon and the construction of the Temple in Jerusalem.

5 See U. Avner, 'Mazzebot Sites in the Negev and Sinai and their Significance,' *Biblical Archeology Today,* 1990.

6 See R.A. Stucky 'Das nabatäische Wohnhaus.'

7 See A. Negev, *Nabatean Archaeology Today.*

Chapter 8

1 Concerning the contents of the papyri of Nessana see A. Negev, *Tempel, Kirchen und Zisternen,* p. 215ff.

2 J. Shereshevski, *Byzantine Urban Settlements,* p. 62.

3 A similar building style from the late first century BC was also found in excavations on the *ez-Zantur* hill in Petra; see J. Shereshevski, *Byzantine Urban Settlements,* p. 79.

4 See R. Rosenthal-Heginbottom, *Die Kirchen von Sobota,* p. 203ff.

5 T. Wiegand, *Sinai.*

6 According to inscriptions, this conversion took place at the end of the seventh century; see A. Negev, 'Greek Inscriptions,' p. 61.

7 For the significance of this ornamental art see pp. 118ff.

8 Concerning the phenomenology of Nabataean names see A. Negev, 'Personal Names.'

9 Y. Baumgartner, 'Mitzpeh Shivta (Mashrafe)' in A. Segal, *Shivta,* (Appendix B).

10 See P. Mayerson, 'The Desert of Southern Palestine,' pp. 160, 170 and Note 1.

11 A. Negev, *Tempel, Kirchen und Zisternen,* p. 204.

Bibliography

Allen, P. M. *A Christian Rosenkreutz Anthology,* New York 1974.

Avi-Yonah, M. and Y. Yadin (Eds.), *Six thousand Years of Art in The Holy Land* [Hebrew], Jerusalem 1990.

Baumgartner, Y. 'Mitzpeh Shivta (Mashrafe)' in A. Segal, *Shivta.*

Beebe, H.K. *The Dromedary Revolution,* Claremont 1990.

Biblical Encyclopedia [Hebrew], Jerusalem 1971.

Biblical Lexicon [Hebrew], Tel Aviv 1965.

Broek, R. van den, *The Myth of Phoenix according to Classical and Early Christian Traditions,* Leiden 1972.

Brünnow, R. and A. v. Domaszewski, *Die Provincia Arabia Petraea,* Vol. I, Strasbourg 1904.

Burckhardt, J.L. *Travels in Syria and the Holy Land,* London 1822.

Casson, L. and E.L. Hettich, *Excavations at Nessana,* Vol. II, Princeton 1950.

Clermont-Ganneau, Ch. *Recueil d'archeologie Orientale,* Paris 1888–1924.

Cruden, A. *A Complete Concordance to the Holy Scriptures,* New York and Edinburgh 1919.

Dalman, G. *Petra und seine Felsheiligtümer,* Leipzig 1908.

Diodorus Siculus, *The Library of History.*

Epiphanios, *Panarion (Adversus Haereisis).*

Evenari, M., L. Shanan and N. Tadmore, *The Negev – The Challenge of a Desert,* Harvard 1982.

Flusser, D. *Jewish Sources in Early Christianity* [Hebrew], Jerusalem 1979.

Gleich, S. von, *Marksteine der Kulturgeschichte,* Stuttgart 1963.

Glueck, N. *Deities and Dolphins,* New York & London 1965.

—, *Rivers in the Desert. A History of the Negev,* New York 1968.

Gwatkin, H.M. *Early Church History,* Vol. II, London 1909.

Hammond, P.C. *The Nabateans: Their History, Culture and Archaeology,* Gothenburg 1973.

Hellenkemper Slies, G. *Die Nabatäer. Erträge einer Austellung in Rheinischen Landesmuseum Bonn, 1978.* Cologne/Bonn 1981.

Heussi, K. *Der Ursprung des Mönchtums,* Tübingen 1936.

Jaeger D. (Ed.), *Christianity in the Holy Land,* Jerusalem 1981.

Jonas, H. *The Gnostic Religion,* Boston 1963.

Josephus, Flavius, *Antiquities of the Jews.*

—, *Contra Apion.*

—, *The Jewish Wars.*

Kasher, A. *Edom, Arabia and Israel* [Hebrew], Jerusalem 1988.

—, (Ed.), *The Great Jewish Revolt,* Jerusalem 1983.

Kedar, Y. *The Ancient Agriculture in the Negev Mountains* [Hebrew], Jerusalem 1967.

Kellner, H.J. *Die Nabatäer. Ein vergessenes Volk am Toten Meer,* (Catalogue for the Munich City Museum prehistoric exhibition) Munich 1970.

Kutzli, R. *Die Bogumilen,* Stuttgart 1977.

Leicht, H. *Kunstgeschichte der Welt,* Zurich 1845.

Licht, J. *The Rule Scroll,* [Hebrew] Jerusalem 1965.

Lindner, M. *Die Könige von Petra. Aufstieg und Niedergang der Nabatäer im biblischen Edom,* Ludwigsburg 1968.

—, (Ed.), *Petra. Neue Ausgrabungen und Entdeckungen,* Munich/Bad Windsheim 1986.

—, (Ed.), *Petra und das Königreich der Nabatäer,* Munich 1970.

McKenzie, J.S. *The Architecture of Petra,* 1990.

Mandel, G. *Il regno di Saba, ultimo paradiso archeologico,* Milan 1976.

Maximus of Tyre, *Philosophoumena.*

Mayerson, P. 'The Desert of Southern Palestine according to Byzantine Sources,' *Proceedings of the American Philosophical Society,* 107, 1963.

Meshorer, Y. *Nabataean Coins,* Jerusalem 1975.

Murray, O. (Ed.), *Sympotika,* Oxford 1994.

Musil, A. *Arabia Petraea,* Vol. II: *Edom,* Vienna 1887/1908.

Negev, A. 'The Architecture of Oboda, Final Report,' *Qedem* 36, Jerusalem 1997.

—, 'Excavations at Elusa' [Hebrew], in *Qadmoniot,* No. 3–4, Jerusalem 1981.

—, 'Greek Inscriptions from the Negev,' *Studium Biblicum Franciscanum, Collectio minor,* No, 25, Jerusalem 1981.

—, *Iconoclastic Nabataean Style,* Unpublished essay.

—, 'The Inscriptions of Wadi Haggag, Sinai,' *Quedem* 6, Jerusalem 1977.

—, *The Land of the Negev* [Hebrew], Tel Aviv 1979.

—, *Masters of the Desert* [Hebrew], Jerusalem 1983.

—, *Nabatean Archaeology Today,* New York & London 1986.

—, *Nabatean Cities in the Negev* [Hebrew], Jerusalem 1988.

—, 'The Nabatean Potter's Workshop of Oboda,' *Acta Rei Cretariae Romanae Fautorum,* Vol. I. Bonn 1974.

—, 'Personal Names in the Nabataean Realm,' *Quedem* 32, Jerusalem 1991.

—, 'Petra,' in *The New Encyclopedia of Archaeological Excavations in the Holy Land* [Hebrew], Jerusalem 1992.

—, *Tempel, Kirchen und Zisternen. Ausgrabungen aus der Wüste Negev. Die Kultur der Nabatäer,* Stuttgart 1983.

—, 'Die Töpferwerkstatt in Oboda (Avdat)' in H.J. Kellner, *Die Nabatäer, ein vergessenes Volk am Toten Meer,* Munich 1970.

Parr, P.J. 'Vierzig Jahre Ausgrabungen in Petra (1929 bis 1969)' in M. Lindner (Ed.), *Petra und das Königreich der Nabatäer.*

Patrich, Joseph, 'Prohibition of a Graven-Image among the Nabataeans' [Hebrew], in *Cathedra* 26, Jerusalem 1983.

Pliny the Elder (Gaius Plinius Secundus) *On Natural History.*

Pliny the Younger (Gaius Plinius Caecilius Secundus) *Epistelarum (Letters).*

Rau, H. *Stilgeschichte der indischen Kunst,* Graz 1986.

Ringel, E. *Das Urchristentum – und wir? Die Katakombenmalerei und der Mysteriencharakter des Christentums,* Dornach 1994.

Rosenthal, F. *Die aramäistische Forschung seit Th. Nöldeke's Veröffentlichungen,* Leiden 1939.

Rosenthal-Heginbottom, R. *Die Kirchen von Sobota und die Dreiapsidenkirchen des Nahen Ostens,* Vol. 7 of *Studien zur spätantiken und frühchristlichen Kunst,* Wiesbaden 1982.

Rost, P. *Die Keilschrifttexte Tiglat-Pilesers,* Vol. III, Leipzig 1893.

Rubin, R. *The Negev as a Settled Land* [Hebrew], Jerusalem 1990.

Ryckmans, J. *L'institution monarchique en Arabie meridionale,* Louvain 1951.

Schaff, Ph. and H. Wace, *Nicene and Post-Nicene Fathers of Christian Church,* Michigan 1954.

Schmitt-Korte, K. 'Die bemahlte nabatäische Keramik: Verbreitung, Typologie und Chronologie,' in M. Lindner (Ed.), *Petra und das Königreich der Nabatäer.*

—, *Die Nabatäer. Ein vergessenes Volk am Toten Meer,* Hanover/Frankfurt 1986.

Segal, A. *Architectural Decoration in Byzantine Shivta, Negev Desert, Israel,* Oxford 1988.

Segal, A. *Architectural Decoration in Byzantine Shivta, Negev Desert, Israel,* Oxford 1988.

—, *Shivta, Portrait of a Byzantine City in the Negev Desert,* Haifa 1986.

Shereshevski, J. *Byzantine Urban Settlements in the Negev Desert,* Beersheba 1991.

Smallwood, A. 'High Priests and Politics in the Roman Israel' [Hebrew], in A. Kasher (Ed.), *The Great Jewish Revolt,* Jerusalem 1983.

Smith, George Adam, *The Historical Geography of the Holy Land,* London 1935.

Steiner, Rudolf, The original German works are numbered as volumes of the *Gesamtausgabe,* (GA).

—, *Building Stones for an Understanding of the Mystery of Golgotha,* London, 1985 (GA 175).

—, *Cosmic Memory,* New York 1985 (GA 11).

—, *Deeper Secrets of Human History,* London & New York 1985 (part of GA 117).

—, *Egyptian Myths and Mysteries,* New York 1971 (GA 106).

—, *The Fifth Gospel,* London 1985 (GA 148).

—, *Karmic Relationships,* Vol. II, London 1974 (GA 236).

—, *Mystery Knowledge and Mystery Centres,* London 1973 (GA 232).

—, *An Outline of Esoteric Science,* New York, 1999 (GA 13).

—, *The Temple Legend. Freemasonry and Related Occult Movements.* London 1985 (GA 93).

—, *Theosophy,* New York, 1994 (GA 9).

—, *World History in the Light of Anthroposophy,* London 1977 (GA 233).

Stephen of Byzantium, *Ethnica.*

Strabo, *Geographica.*

Stucky, R.A. 'Das nabatäische Wohnhaus und das urbanistische System der Wohnquartiere in Petra,' in *Antike Kunst,* 35, 1992.

Suda Lexicon. Tenth century Byzantine literary encyclopedia.

Tzaferis, V. *Christian Symbols of the Fourth Century and the Church Fathers,* Diss., Jerusalem 1971.

Weber, Thomas and Robert Wenning (Eds.), *Petra. Antike Felstadt zwischen arabischer Tradition und griechischer Norm,* Mainz 1997.

Welburn, Andrew, *The Beginnings of Christianity,* Edinburgh 1991.

Wenning, R. *Die Nabatäer — Denkmäler und Geschichte. Eine Bestandaufnahme des archäologischen Befundes,* Gottingen 1987.

Wiegand, T. *Sinai,* Berlin and Leizpig 1920.

Yassif, E. *The Tales of Ben Sira in the Middle Ages* [Hebrew], Jerusalem 1984.

Zayadine, F. 'Die Felsenarchitektur Petras,' in M. Lindner (Ed.), *Petra.*

—, 'Die Götter der Nabatäer' in M. Lindner (Ed.) *Petra.*

—, (Ed.) *Petra and the Caravan Cities,* Amman 1990.

Acknowledgments

American Center for Oriental Research, Amman, Figures 49, 50; Werner Braun, Jerusalem, Figure 10; Manfred Christ, Stuttgart, Figures 1, 2; Dr Richard Cleave, Rohr Productions Ltd, Nikosia, Figures 3, 23, 33, 34, 35, 36, 38, 54, 57; Nelson Glueck, *Deities and Dolphins,* Figure 47; Adolf Grohmann, *Kulturgeschichte des alten Orients,* Munich 1963, Figure 6; Erich Lessing, Vienna, Figure 4; Avraham Negev, *Tempel, Kirchen und Zisterne,* Figure 5; Avraham Negev, 'The late Hellenistic and early Roman Pottery,' *Qedem* 22, Jerusalem 1986, Figures 22, 24, 31; Rolf Pawlowsky, Neustadt/W., Figures 14, 41, 42, 43, 44, 46, 48, 51; Renate Rosenthal-Heginbottom, *Die Kirchen von Sobota,* Figures 18, 27, 67; Arthur Segal, Shivta, Figures 20, 52, 61; Christine Talker-Jordanis, Figures 7, 11, 12, 13, 17, 29, 30; Jane Taylor, Amman, Figures 28, 39, 45.

Index